# Artificial Intelligence and Emerging Technologies in International Relations

**Other World Scientific Titles by the Author**

*Causality, Correlation and Artificial Intelligence for Rational Decision Making*
ISBN: 978-981-4630-86-3

*Handbook of Machine Learning*
*Volume 1: Foundation of Artificial Intelligence*
ISBN: 978-981-3271-22-7

*Handbook of Machine Learning*
*Volume 2: Optimization and Decision Making*
ISBN: 978-981-120-566-8

# Artificial Intelligence and Emerging Technologies in International Relations

## Bhaso Ndzendze
## Tshilidzi Marwala

University of Johannesburg, South Africa

**World Scientific**

NEW JERSEY · LONDON · SINGAPORE · BEIJING · SHANGHAI · HONG KONG · TAIPEI · CHENNAI · TOKYO

*Published by*

World Scientific Publishing Co. Pte. Ltd.

5 Toh Tuck Link, Singapore 596224

*USA office:* 27 Warren Street, Suite 401-402, Hackensack, NJ 07601

*UK office:* 57 Shelton Street, Covent Garden, London WC2H 9HE

**Library of Congress Cataloging-in-Publication Data**
Names: Ndzendze, Bhaso, author. | Marwala, Tshilidzi, 1971– author.
Title: Artificial intelligence and emerging technologies in international relations /
    Bhaso Ndzendze, Tshilidzi Marwala.
Description: Hackensack, New Jersey : World Scientific, [2021] |
    Includes bibliographical references and index.
Identifiers: LCCN 2020055715 | ISBN 9789811234545 (hardcover) |
    ISBN 9789811234552 (ebook for institutions) | ISBN 9789811234569 (ebook for individuals)
Subjects: LCSH: Technology and international relations. |
    Artificial intelligence--Political aspects. | Geopolitics.
Classification: LCC JZ1254 .N47 2021 | DDC 327--dc23
LC record available at https://lccn.loc.gov/2020055715

**British Library Cataloguing-in-Publication Data**
A catalogue record for this book is available from the British Library.

For any available supplementary material, please visit
https://www.worldscientific.com/worldscibooks/10.1142/12216#t=suppl

Typeset by Stallion Press
Email: enquiries@stallionpress.com

Printed in Singapore

# Preface

Seismic changes are sweeping the globe because of the Fourth Industrial Revolution (4IR). The 4IR is an era where technologies are becoming intelligent and thus blurring the lines between the cyber, physical and biological spaces. The technologies that are driving these changes include Artificial Intelligence, Blockchain and Internet of Things. These technologies are transforming every sphere of human activity and interaction; no sphere is left untouched — from security threats, to commercial flows, to international law. Yet changes of a technological nature are not a new phenomenon. Indeed, the present world is a result of changes which took place in the past.

This text is an overview of technology dynamics in International Relations (IR). In seven chapters, this book reviews the interconnectedness between technology and the international political economy. The book is particularly concerned with the development, deployment, transfer, management and disposal of technologies in historical and contemporary perspective. It begins with the life cycles of technologies (Chapter 2) before examining internationally-produced domestic dilemmas and developments (Chapters 3–5) and the role technology plays in IR as international actors seek to maximize the gains and minimize the downsides of technology (Chapters 6–8). In this arena, technology emerges as a subject of diplomacy, as well as its catalyst and increasingly diplomacy's focal point in terms of transnational issues.

# Acknowledgements

We wish to express our appreciation to the incredible staff at World Scientific for their incredible support throughout the writing and production of this book. Our editor Yu Shan Tay played a critical role in all the various stages of the project, from proposal to manuscript to the production of the book. Comments by the anonymous reviewers polished the work further. We are thankful for their inputs.

As a token of our appreciation, this book is dedicated to the staff and students of the University of Johannesburg, who have shown resilience and adaptability throughout the difficulties and challenges brought on by the COVID-19 pandemic. Their embrace of, and critical engagement with, the various aspects of the 4IR has provided the environment needed for the pursuit of the ideas explored in this volume.

Special thanks in this regard also goes to our students in the POL8X27 group (Technology Dynamics in International Relations) class of 2020, from whose lectures many elements of this book were developed or further honed. Their dedication and enthusiasm towards the module in the face of unprecedented conditions was inspiring.

Bhaso Ndzendze, PhD and Tshilidzi Marwala, PhD
Johannesburg
April 2021

# Contents

# List of Abbreviations

| | |
|---|---|
| 2IR | Second Industrial Revolution |
| 3IR | Third Industrial Revolution |
| 4IR | Fourth Industrial Revolution |
| 4GW | Fourth Generation Warfare |
| 5G | Fifth generation connectivity |
| ABM | Agent-Based Model |
| AI | Artificial Intelligence |
| AfDB | African Development Bank |
| AU | African Union |
| AIIB | Asian Infrastructure Investment Bank |
| BERD | Business expenditure on research and development |
| BRI | Belt and Road Initiative |
| BRICS | Brazil, Russia, India, China and South Africa |
| CIA | Central Intelligence Agency |
| DFH | Demand-following hypothesis |
| DTI | Development of Telecommunications Infrastructure |
| EU | European Union |
| FBH | Feedback hypothesis |
| FDI | Foreign Direct Investment |
| FVEY | Five Eyes |
| GDP | Gross Domestic Product |
| GDPR | General Data Protection Regulation |
| GERD | Government expenditure on research and development |
| GME | Goods Market Efficiency |
| GSOMIA | General Security of Military Information Agreement |
| GVC | Global value chain |
| HE | Higher education |
| IAEA | International Atomic Energy Agency |
| IDEA | Institute for Democracy and Electoral Assistance |
| ICJ | International Court of Justice |
| ICT | Information and Communications Technology |

| IoT | Internet of Things |
| IPE | International Political Economy |
| IP | Intellectual Property |
| IR | International Relations |
| ITU | International Telecommunications Union (ITU) |
| IW | Information warfare |
| LDC | Less Developed Country |
| ML | Machine Learning |
| MNC | Multinational Corporation |
| MNE | Multinational enterprise |
| NATO | North Atlantic Treaty Organisation |
| NBER | National Bureau of Economic Research |
| NLH | Neutrality hypothesis |
| NLP | Natural Language Processing |
| NPT | Non-Proliferation Treaty |
| NTI | Nuclear Threat Initiative |
| OAU | Organisation of African Unity |
| OECD | Organization of Economic Cooperation and Development |
| OFDI | Outward foreign direct investment |
| OSS | Open source software |
| PPP | Purchasing power parity |
| PRC | People's Republic of China |
| R&D | Research and Development |
| SAGW | Surface-to-air guided weapon |
| SCO | Shanghai Cooperation Organisation |
| SDO | Standards Development Organisations |
| SDGs | Sustainable Development Goals |
| SME | Small and medium enterprise |
| STEM | Science, technology, engineering and mathematics |
| STI | Science, Technology and Innovation |
| SLH | Supply-leading hypothesis |
| TAN | Transnational Advocacy Networks |
| UKUSA | UK, US and Australia |
| UN | United Nations |
| UNCTAD | United Nations Conference on Trade and Development |
| USSR | Union of Soviet Socialist Republics |
| WEF | World Economic Forum |

| | |
|---|---|
| WHO | World Health Organisation |
| WIPO | World Intellectual Property Organisation |
| WSIS | World Summit on the Information Society |
| WWI | World War I |
| WWII | World War II |

# List of Figures

# List of Tables

# Introduction: Artificial Intelligence and Other Emerging Technologies

On 12 September 1962, American president John F. Kennedy gave an address at Rice University in Texas in which he summed-up the history of human technical advancement in allegorical terms, stating that if the 50,000 years of recorded human history were to be condensed into five decades, then:

> "The printing press came this year, and then less than two months ago, during this whole 50-year span of human history, the steam engine provided a new source of power. Newton explored the meaning of gravity. Last month electric lights and telephones and automobiles and airplanes became available. Only last week did we develop penicillin and television and nuclear power."

Given the backdrop of his speech — the announcement of America's intention to go to the moon within the end of the 1960s — he added that "now if America's new spacecraft succeeds in reaching Venus, we will have literally reached the stars before midnight tonight. This is a breathtaking pace, and such a pace cannot help but create new ills as it dispels old, new ignorance, new problems, [and] new dangers." Observations of new dangers and prospects of higher productivity once more abound in present times as seismic changes again sweep the globe at breathtaking pace. At the root of these are technological transformations impacting every sphere of human activity and interaction; no sphere is left untouched — from security threats to commercial flows and even international law. Yet changes of a technological nature are not a new phenomenon. Indeed, the present world is a result of changes which took place in the past along certain trajectories whose influence persists and can be discerned today.

These nodes of human development and what they represent have sparked much debate; there is contestation about the sort of outcomes they bring about, and at the same time about what sorts of domestic institutions are needed for innovation of the good sort to take shape. Also debated is how to achieve the ideal human-machine interface. These are areas of much importance and of unprecedented relevance to the social sciences research agenda, including (and perhaps especially) International Relations (IR). This book seeks to understand these from such a perspective. In so doing we traverse the landscape in terms of theoretical frameworks for thinking about technology in societal terms at the national, transnational, regional and international levels, while also determining the factors which have allowed some countries to emerge at the top of technology indicators. This allows us to better understand ongoing trends in the new technologies and to modestly prognosticate the future impact of Artificial Intelligence (AI) and other emerging technologies and to identify the threats and opportunities they represent for development cooperation, regional integration, diplomatic engagement and conflict.

One of the key contributions of this book is a clear assessment of the implications of AI and other emerging technologies for these IR processes. We observe the potential of these to potentially upend much of the post-Cold War era of globalisation, including by posing a threat to the current state of interdependence which has been the basis of the era of relative peace since World War II (WWII). On the other hand, issues such as heightened energy consumption will require some form of global cooperation, while 4IR technologies such as Big Data and blockchain can potentially enable democracy and accountability, despite having mainly facilitated populism so far. As the field of International Relations engages more with these technologies, clarity in methodological analysis will be essential in order to present cogent studies that take stock of big questions in an empirical manner as its scholars embark on a new phase of interdisciplinary analysis.

In this chapter we briefly distill what we mean by emerging technologies, before turning to an overview of the present state of IR literature on AI and other emerging technologies. We then present the book's key thematic contributions before giving a layout of the various chapters in this volume.

## 1.1 Emerging Technologies

These technologies that are changing the world are collectively called the Fourth Industrial Revolution (4IR). The 4IR was preceded by the Third Industrial Revolution (3IR) which introduced the electronic age through the discovery of a transistor. The 3IR was preceded by the Second Industrial

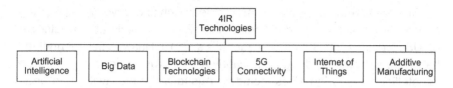

Fig. 1.1. Technologies defining the 4IR.

Revolution (2IR) which was catalyzed by the developments in electromagnetism that led to the invention of electricity and the electric motor. These ushered mass production of goods and services. The 2IR was preceded by the first industrial revolution which used the steam engine for transportation as well as to power machines in the production of goods and services (Marwala, 2020; Doorsamy *et al.*, 2020). The defining technologies of the 4IR that have a productive component and an IR interface are summarized in Fig. 1.1 and include Artificial Intelligence, 3D printing (also known as additive manufacturing), new materials (such as graphene), the Internet of Things (IoT), and Blockchain (with cryptocurrencies having a total cumulative value of US$237 billion in 2020 [Fox, 2020]).

The determined baseline for consumer market adoption of these technologies for societies differ, but a widely adopted one is 10% for wearables that are connected to the Internet, Gross Domestic Product (GDP) that is stored in Blockchain technology and driverless cars, while it is 30% for corporate audits being conducted by AI (Schwab, 2016: 26). In other words, at least some tenth of a society must be making use of the given technology and almost a third of its GDP must be in the form of Blockchain for it to be regarded as having sufficiently penetrated the critical mass or reached a tipping point. This book's regard of these technologies as being mainly emerging rather than established stems from their limited reach as well as the extensive — indeed exponential — rate with which new and farther-reaching applications are being developed as indicated by the pace of registration of new patents in offices globally (though, importantly, at an uneven rate among various countries). The World Intellectual Property Organisation (WIPO) observes massive upticks in funding coming from governments and (even more) from the private sectors. These upticks are also indicative of immense collaboration across borders. In the same vein, however, they are characterised by competition most starkly between the US and China. This geopolitical rivalry may be the most pronounced, but it is by far not the only one.

China and Australia have seen their Research and Development (R&D) cooperation reach a fractured point since 2019, partially as an outcome of US pressure on the latter. Australia's 2019 Huawei 5G technology ban was, in other words, greatly catalysed by Washington's pressure on its intelligence-sharing allies including Australia but the rivalry has been decades in the making due to public and political ambivalence towards Australia's economic entanglement with China, focused on the country's human rights record as well as competition over regional hegemony in the Asia-Pacific.

In another tussle in which technology has been infused is the India–China rivalry, which has seen the former ban over 58 Chinese apps following a border clash in June 2020 in which some 20 Indian soldiers were killed. In September 2020, the number of banned apps was increased to 118 (Agence France-Presse, 2020). The most famous among these apps was TikTok. Another fellow Brazil, Russia, India, China and South Africa (BRICS) member with whom China has been involved in a technology dispute is Russia, which has claimed that China duplicated its military technologies.

The Chief of Intellectual Property Projects of Russian defense technology conglomerate Rostec said in December 2019 that "unauthorized copying of our equipment abroad is a huge problem. There have been 500 such cases over the past 17 years," adding that "China alone has copied aircraft engines, Sukhoi planes, deck jets, air defense systems, portable air defense missiles, and analogs of the Pantsir medium-range surface-to-air systems" (Simes, 2020). In the early 1990s, the People's Republic of China (PRC) had also purchased Russia's Su-27 fighter jets and S-300 missile systems and by 1995 had used these as templates for developing its own J-11 fighter jet and HQ-9 surface-to-air guided weapon (SAGW). Despite (or indeed possibly due to) Russia accounting for 70% of Chinese military imports over the 2015–2019 period, Moscow has been disincentivised from taking a punitive stance towards Chinese reverse engineering of its technology — the opportunity cost represented from forfeiting such a market and geopolitical advantages is simply too high. "Today Russia has come to accept China's technology theft as the inevitable price of doing business with its southern neighbor," concludes Vasily Kashin, a Russian Academy of Science senior fellow (Simes, 2020). While in the 1990s Russia successfully pressed China to purchase its weapons in bulk quantities (as opposed to only a few samples which could be reverse engineered) and to pay royalties when such reverse engineering had taken place, this is no longer the case. A large part of this is partially attributable to the decline in Chinese imports which emanated from these conditions (with Russian manufactures accounting for a mere 8.7% of Beijing's imports in 2012). The great catalyst for the resurgence in arms imports was the Crimean Crisis of 2014[1] and the resultant sanctions from the West, which pushed Russia towards China. This is exemplary of political developments shaping the supply and demand dynamics of technology.

Likewise, historical events can re-emerge and bring into jeopardy any normalcy in technological value chains. Though Japan and South Korea have experienced a normalisation of their relations in 1965, South Korea's insistence on Japanese atonement for having colonised it in 1910 and for treatment of its population during WWII have been variously responded to by successive Japanese prime ministers. The relationship is also complicated by maritime disputes. The Shinzo Abe period has seen a growth in Japanese nationalism, with the country's foreign representatives less inclined to atonement. This resulted in a diplomatic tussle which began in 2018 when South Korean activists constructed a statue commemorating victims of Japan during WWII outside the Japanese consulate in Busan, South Korea. Japan protested that this was against the Vienna Convention which dictates diplomatic courtesy by host countries. Korean citizens were bolstered by a 2019 judgement by the country's Supreme Court which allowed them to sue the Japanese government for war-time labour in their capacity as individuals. Many proceeded to do so. Seeing this as endorsed by the government in Seoul Japan refused to provide critical semiconductors to South Korea's Samsung, which in turn influenced South Korea's decision to cut off the 2016-signed General Security of Military Information Agreement (GSOMIA). In this regard, progress in the technology sphere always remains vulnerable to the caprice of human affairs and politics despite the promise of absolute and apolitical rationality represented by the successive industrial revolutions.

Short of a diplomatic tussle but still intense are the relations between the European Union (EU) and US technology companies over policy. This has resulted in over US$9.5 billion being paid in fines by Google since 2017 on account of violating antitrust laws by ensuring its position in the digital advertising market through denying competitors' advertisements prominence in its search results. There are ongoing investigations by the EU into Amazon

---

[1]This is in reference to the Russian government's incorporation of Crimea, hirtherto a part of Ukraine, in 2014 in a manner that was regarded as illegal by the EU and the US, though Russia claimed that it was through popular will.

(for reportedly alleged anticompetitive standards in its e-commerce market-place), Apple (for anticompetitive practices towards music streaming competitor Spotify) and Facebook (for denying users control over their personal data in its flagship social network, as well as in other platforms it owns, especially Instagram and WhatsApp) with US$2 billion on the line at the time of writing. These influential tech giants are being sued for failure to comply with the General Data Protection Regulation (GDPR) which went into effect in 2018. One reason the EU — as opposed to other regions (including the US) — has succeeded in suing these tech giants has reportedly been the fact that "[it is] easier to prove market dominance under EU legal standards" than in other jurisdictions (Schulze, 2019).

Studies show an ongoing battle for influence over international Standards Development Organisations (SDOs), particularly the United Nations' International Telecommunications Union (ITU), to determine and re-shape the standards, ethics and norms which have governed the Internet for decades. In their *Journal of Cyber Policy* article, Hoffman, Lazanski and Taylor caution that this could lead to the internet being divided into two (Hoffmann *et al.*, 2020: 239).

### 1.1.1 *Artificial Intelligence*

Artificial Intelligence, perhaps the defining technology of the 4IR, is not a singular industry or field of study and research. Rather it refers to a variety of algorithm-based machines and processes which can act autonomously, learning as they do so through Machine Learning (ML) and in so doing appear to mimic the cognitive as well as behavioural patterns of human beings (AI in IR Project, 2020; Marwala, 2018; Marwala and Leke, 2019). Within AI, there are specialised areas of robotics, Natural Language Processing (NLP) and ML. The last of these three is the leading area of growth, with some 60% of funding in AI being in ML. Briefly, the ML value chain consists of the following steps: (1) Data collection; (2) Data storage; (3) Data preparation; (4) Algorithm training, and (5) Application development. These stages involve (1) obtaining raw data; (2) placing these raw data in data centers; (3) conversion, formatting and labelling of these raw data; (4) configuring an algorithm that can make predictions based on the data; and (5) converting these algorithmic predictions into commercial products and applications such as software with installations in mobile apps, medical diagnostic tools, military equipment, geospatial observation and self-driving automobiles.

At the same time, 5G is prognosticated to be a key infrastructural technology. The convergence of these technologies provides the basis for the observations and predictions about the future ubiquity of these 4IR technologies. Thus, many identify the exceptional and growing computational power and Big Data as providing the distinguishing factor of the current age of AI from previous "AI winters" in which the technology had experienced significant setbacks in funding (roughly from 1974 to 1980, and again from 1987 to 1993).

### 1.1.2 *The Internet of Things*

The Internet of Things refers to the connectivity among devices through which they have a physical-digital interface with the use of sensors. Among the applications of the IoT are the digital integration of homes, which in turn can be ratcheted up to the level of cities with applications in security, energy optimisation and traffic regulation, among others. In other words, this technology is set to become one of the central infrastructures of the future. For international affairs, this has implications for such factors as travel, tourism, anti-terror efforts and supply chains. The latter point is made more apparent when taking into account the effects of the IoT on the global value chain once applied to smart factories. These are factories which are able to work productively in unison with one another in real time. This is the basis for Manufacturing 4.0. One of the leading companies is Swedish electronics giant Ericsson which utilises self-operating screwdrivers, communicating workstations, and geo-tracked (remotely managed) steel pallets and fire extinguishers. "By automating and streamlining production, maintenance, and with immersed data analysis," the company's Chinese based operations states that it sees savings through "increased efficiency, fewer human errors, increased reliability, nearly zero downtime, and improved service life for tools and equipment" (Ericsson Panda, 2020).

### 1.1.3 *5G Connectivity*

5G (or fifth-generation connectivity) refers to a nascent telecommunications technology which will facilitate faster connections — up to 100 gigabits per second. This technology, which is currently led by China and the US operates through dedicated networking that is used by specific users for specific purposes through the phenomenon of network slicing. Thus instead of the prevalent method of telecommunications towers being located in locales that serve wide areas, as is the case with older generations of technology such as 4G, the delivery of 5G hubs (i.e., end-to-end networks put in place by service providers for customers) are located in proximity to users (Marwala, 2020: 102). Some specific types of nodes of this network slicing can include traffic regulation, machine to machine interaction (as seen with the Ericsson factories previously mentioned), entertainment and medical infrastructure. Diplomatic standoffs have taken place between the US and its allies on one hand, and the PRC on the other, with the main issue being Chinese tech giant Huawei's provision of 5G infrastructure to countries with whom the US has intelligence sharing agreements. Future tiffs of this kind are widely anticipated in coming years and decades, as governments seek to protect their interests as well as reach new markets first. The opposite is just as true, with the countries of the European Union having issued an AI cooperation strategy in 2020, while the World Health Organization looks to make medical AI more available and ethical. The factors which lead to either outcome (including the interests at play and the rationales for the alternatives explored and selected) — as well as the results either approach yields for societies, individual countries, regions and the world as a whole — are the impetus behind this book.

## 1.2 Literature

Naturally, technologies can be understood as a domestic economic phenomenon: they are indicators of successful innovation and industrial policies, infrastructural development and even nation-building. Cast in these terms, technology is both a catalyst and an outcome of a nation's economic development trajectory. Because of this, moreover, it has a global economic component. In 2007, for example, the World Bank observed that, broadly speaking, much of the inequality among countries stems from gaps in productivity, a large portion of which in turn can be deducted from differing (i.e., inequitable) levels of access to technology among countries.

Figure 1.2, for example, demonstrates the lag between Ghana and South Korea from 1960–2005. These two economies — which started off from a relatively similar base in terms of GDP (US$1.217 billion for Ghana and US$3.9 billion for South Korea) and GDP per capita (US$183 for Ghana and US$158 for South Korea) — have since gone on to observe a divergent path in favour of the East Asian country. By 2019, Ghana had a nominal GDP of US$65 billion and a GDP per capita of US$2,202, while South Korea's GDP was US$1.6 trillion with a GDP per capita of more than US$31,000.

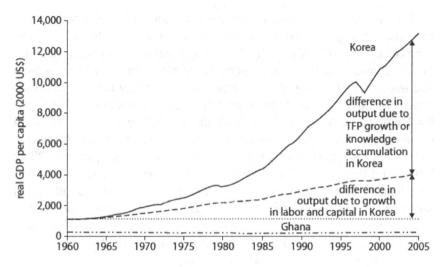

Fig. 1.2.   Innovation and productivity gap: Ghana and South Korea, 1960–2005.
*Source*: The World Bank (2007).
*Note*: TPF = total factor productivity.

In this sense, technology can act as a determinant (predictor) and sig-nifier of international Foreign Direct Investment (FDI) flows, with countries which enjoy technological advantage being more likely to gain greater FDI gains precisely for this reason. In turn, the inflows of this FDI can be put to use through investing in capital inputs. These two factors are crucial to the attainment of the so-called virtuous circle; the process whereby inputs can be put to use to routinise efficiency and ensure growth. In line with this, it can act as a predictor of other processes that preoccupy policymak-ers at the national and international levels. Technologies bring possibilities of destabilisation of technology value chains, while also shaping security thinking as possession of certain technologies determine the likelihood of one state winning a conflict over another. On the other hand, countries in the developing world are concerned with the retention of technically tal-ented and educated segments of its population, a process known as "brain drain" through which countries lose many skilled citizens.

There is thus a clear research mandate for scholars of International Relations. Indeed, the mutual interaction between technology and IR dom-inates much of the field's subject: transnational history. To a large degree, technologies partially determine how we understand the history of IR and how we theorise about its processes. These are briefly discussed in turn.

The Age of Exploration, the process through which European countries undertook global discovery from the 1400s to the 17th century, was a product of the Renaissance, Scientific Revolution and the Enlightenment in Europe. Insights on astronomy led to more efficiency for navigation and eventuated into the global system we have today through colonisation and the globalisation of the Westphalian system which emanated from the Thirty Years' War of 1618 to 1648; the war itself was a product of the Renaissance and a major episode in the history of military technology with the large-scale switch from swords to guns (Ogilvie, 1996; Parrott, 2012; Naudé and Nagler, 2017). In the main, through wars of conquest including colonisation, was a technological phenomenon; possession of advanced weaponry placed the European colonialists in a position of advantage against local populations in Africa, Australia, Asia and the Americas. Here, crucially, weapons allowed European armies to compensate for their lower numbers in manpower (Strachan, 2005: 112).

Technological advancements brought on by the 2IR subsequently introduced Europe and other parts of the globe to industrialised total war during WWI (1914–1919). The war saw the debut, amongst others, of large-scale use of armoured tanks, planes and wireless radio communication which transformed the logistical character of war. It also transformed the scale and lethality of war. This war was followed by a more destructive one, with WWII brought to a close by the deployment of the nuclear bomb in Japan by the US in August 1945. The proliferation of "the Bomb", as it came to be known, from the US to its ideological rival, the USSR, in turn gave rise to the concept of mutually assured destruction which would undergird the Cold War (Waltz, 1981), while also continuing to cause restraint between the US and China, the US and Russia, China and India, Pakistan and India, and even other countries in alliance with any of the nuclear states in the North Atlantic Treaty Organization to this day.

Another crucial technological development that reshaped IR was the Internet which entered mainstream use in the 1990s and has since come to be regarded as a "global highway" and a bedrock of international transactions, through simplifying interstate trade, communication, education and cultural consumption. A direct byproduct of the technical developments has been the environmental impact of more efficient production, which has global implications. As such, then, technology has policy and theoretical implications for IR as it presents new avenues for analysis in the subject's main branches: international economics, diplomacy and war.

How will AI and other emerging technologies change why and how states fight? Will it present new *casus belli*, new forms of pressure, new forms of command and control in combat? And what new opportunities and challenges will they present in the way of diplomacy? Do they imbue new meanings of power and new channels of interaction? These, and many others that emerge frequently, are the questions which have come into the fore in the literature.

Over the past number of years, there has been a litany of interesting and well-considered books on technology and IR, signifying a growing interest by political scientists in technology. Many of these have consisted of reports and studies published by think tanks and associations, such as Chatham House and the Belfer Center at Harvard University. While well-considered and providing useful insights, these are usually seized by a particular topic, and from the perspective of the given countries' foreign policies. On the other hand, journal articles have tended to be specialist-oriented and inaccessible. Some excellent book-length volumes include the following. *Power, Information Technology, and International Relations Theory: The Power and Politics of US Foreign Policy and the Internet* by D. McCarthy published in 2015, "combines analyses of global material culture and international relation theory, to reconsider how technology is understood as a form of social power." However, this volume is confined mainly to the Internet, and is written from a US foreign policy perspective, and thus excludes much of what the present volume is set to engage with. *New Technologies as a Factor of International Relations* by Monika Szkarłat and Katarzyna Mojska published in 2016 has contributions "drawn from different disciplines, including political science, international relations, sociology, economy, law, biochemistry and bioethics, as well as from different locations, including Poland, the US, Brazil and Israel." Significantly, the book gives a theoretical-empirical analysis of technological development on contemporary international relations. Read alongside each other, a reader of this and the Szkarłat-Mojska volume can walk away with a greater sense of the ubiquity of technology in International Relations not only among countries, but on the entire contemporary global system. *Technology and International Relations: Challenges for the 21st Century* by Bhaskar Balakrishnan published in 2017, begins with the past before getting to the present century, examining science/technology sectors with a view to extract conclusions about the role of diplomacy in the management of these fast-moving and implicative sectors. The book showcases technology as both a subject and catalyst of diplomacy using a sectoral analysis. Excellently written and well-researched, however, the book pins most of its focus on diplomacy. Our own volume delves into diplomacy, and in so doing highlights the perspectives of the Global South, but also notes where it may fall short. Overall, our volume hopes to feature diplomacy as one cog among many in the technology-IR nexus by showcasing other means of cooperation as well as scenarios in which it is unsurmountable, using theoretical frameworks. At the same time, it improves on the sectoral approach taken in Balakrishnan's book.

In *Future War,* Robert H. Latiff charts ways in which the changing nature of war and the weapons technologies used to fight them are coming into being, "seeking to describe the ramifications of those changes and what it will mean in the future to be a soldier." Latiff also indicates that the fortunes of countries are inextricably intertwined to its national defense in this coming age, and therefore the need for citizens to understand the importance of when, how and according to what rules we fight. Our volume will make use of some of the insights which Latiff, a retired Major General with involvement in the US Army and NORAD, gets close to but stops short of making by expanding and testing the global implications of the hypotheses he advances (such as civilian involvement, the military-industrial complex and the life cycles of specific technologies) beyond the US, which is his primary focus. *Technology and Agency in International Relations (Emerging Technologies, Ethics and International Affairs)* by Marijn Hoijtink and Matthias Leese published in 2019 looks at "insights from science and technology studies (STS), assemblage theory and new materialism," and investigates "how international politics are made possible, knowable, and durable by and through technology." In this regard, this volume is a major contribution to the scholars in this emerging field. In this volume we aim to be much more interdisciplinary in scope.

This text will prime students for engagement with present and future issues in conflict resolution, international financial flows, policy studies, foreign policymaking and international law in the context of major shifts in the modern world. The fundamental aim of this text is to assist the reader to derive a working understanding of the nature of developments in the technological sectors through the lenses of IR and political science both in terms of their antecedents and the outcomes they produce.

In the seven upcoming chapters we delve into the interaction between technology and international politics and international political economy and, in the conclusion, we ponder ways in which the emerging fundamental questions may be engaged with by academia. This book, then, is particularly concerned with the development, deployment, transfer, management and disposal of technologies in historical and contemporary perspective. In Chapter 2, we review the development of technology in historical perspective. We understand the relationship between necessity and invention in the long durée of human history. This historical arc is linked with contemporary developments and differences between countries. Having encountered interstate differences in the second chapter, in Chapter 3, we look at the various policies that lead to flows of technologies from developed societies to late developers, including through trade and FDI. In Chapter 4, we review the effect of domestic policies on the domestic development of technologies through R&D. Particularly assessed is the academic literature on the role of institutions, both formal and informal. Conversely the effect of technology on political interfaces is examined. In Chapter 5, the development of infrastructure and the overall aim of industrialisation among various countries are empirically reviewed while being problematised. In Chapter 6, we look at the historical role of technology in war between countries and the effect of new technologies on the future of interstate conflict. While this chapter looks at the role of technology in conflict situations, in Chapter 7, we review the role of technology in cooperative behavior, namely in integration among states in the same geographical location. In Chapter 8, we review the conduct of diplomacy in the age of digitisation, and in turn scientific diplomacy for the 4IR. Finally, the chapter is an analysis of technology as both a tool of diplomacy as well as technology as an object of diplomatic interaction. Figure 1.3 briefly outlines the chapter-specific relevance of AI and the other emerging technologies.

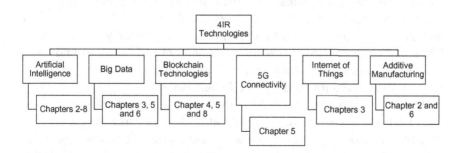

Fig. 1.3.    Chapter breakdown of specific technologies.

## 1.3   Fundamentals and Patterns

The analyses conducted in the forthcoming chapters lead us to establish the themes of fundamentals and patterns. Essentially, the world is defined by inequalities in technological capabilities both between as well as within countries. The fundamentals, explored in Chapters 2 and 3, are based on the historical origins and contemporary policies that sustain and self-reproduce the nature of these inequities. Importantly, the research finds that there is no single set of policies that work. Instead, in the group of innovative societies, there are a variety of successful policies that tech sector companies and entrepreneurs make use of. They take advantage of this variety on a global scale in this era of moving global capital. This is perhaps reflected most clearly in the multiplicity of yardsticks used to measure the technological readiness of countries and their business synergy implications. Nevertheless, key features define societies which dominate the globe in terms of the technology global value chain to take semiconductors, consumer electronics, capital inputs and digital platforms as proxies. These countries are, in turn, set to dominate the globe in terms of AI and other emerging technologies.

In terms of the second theme (i.e., patterns), the book determines a historical shift in terms of technology and innovation, with increased participation and leadership in some areas in the traditional Global South or the former Third World (i.e., non-OECD [the Organization for Economic Cooperation and Development] countries). Most notably, China now accounts for about half of all new patents in 2018 with the Belt and Road Initiative (BRI), an infrastructure rollout on an unprecedented global scale. Moreover, there is a pattern emerging through which non-state actors are coming to the fore due to their leadership in R&D and the implications of developments in the commercial spheres for war, diplomacy, regional integration and global environmental sustainability and energy security, particularly in terms of electronic waste (e-waste) management and balances and compromises on nuclear proliferation and its peaceable applications per International Atomic Energy Agency (IAEA) guidelines.

Overall, this text not only looks at the life cycles of technologies (Chapter 2) but is also an examination of internationally-produced domestic dilemmas and developments (Chapters 2–4) and of the role technology plays in IR as international actors seek to maximize the gains and minimize the downsides of technology (Chapters 5–7). In this arena, technology emerges as a subject of diplomacy (e.g., science and technology diplomacy), as well as its catalyst and increasingly diplomacy's main transnational issue.

# References

AI in IR Project. 2020. "AI in IR?," *AI in IR*. URL: https://aiinir.org/ai (Accessed: 23 November 2020).

Agence France-Presse. 2020. "India bans 118 Chinese apps, accusing companies of stealing data," *The Guardian*. URL: https://www.theguardian.com/world/2020/sep/03/india-bans-118-chinese-apps-accusing-companies-of-stealing-data (Accessed: 23 September 2020).

Doorsamy, Wesley, Sena Paul, Babu and Marwala, Tshilidzi (Editors). 2020. *The Disruptive Fourth Industrial Revolution — Technology, Society and Beyond*. Geneva, Switzerland: Springer Nature.

Fox, Matthew. 2020. "Crypto market grows by $13 billion as bitcoin breaks the $10,000 threshold for the first time since February," *Business Insider*. URL: https://markets.businessinsider.com/currencies/news/bitcoin-price-crypto-market-grows-billions-breaks-threshold-value-total-2020-5-1029182471 (Accessed: 20 September 2020).

Hoffmann, Stacie, Lazanski, Dominique, and Taylor, Emily. 2020. "Standardising the splinternet: how China's technical standards could fragment the internet," *Journal of Cyber Policy*, 5(2), 239–264.

Marwala, Tshilidzi. 2020. *Closing the Gap: The Fourth Industrial Revolution in Africa*. Johannesburg: Macmillan.

Marwala, Tshilidzi. 2018. *Handbook of Machine Learning: Foundation of Artificial Intelligence*, Volume 1. Singapore: World Scientific.

Marwala, Tshilidzi and Leke, Collins. 2019. *Handbook of Machine Learning: Optimization and Decision Making*, Vol. 2. World Scientific Publication.

Naudé, Wim and Nagler, Paula. 2017. "Technological Innovation and Inclusive Growth in Germany," No. 11194, Institute of Labor Economics. URL: http://ftp.iza.org/dp11194.pdf (Accessed: 24 September 2020).

Ogilvie, Sheilagh. 1996. "The Beginnings of Industrialization," in Ogilvie, Sheilagh., editor, *Germany: A New Social and Economic History, Vol. II: 1630–1800*. London: Hodder Arnold.

Parrott, David. 2012. *The Business of War: Military Enterprise and Military Revolution in Early Modern Europe*. Cambridge: Cambridge University Press.

Schwab, Klaus. 2016. *The Fourth Industrial Revolution*. London: Portfolio Penguin.

Schulze, Elizabeth. 2020. "If you want to know what a US tech crackdown may look like, check out what Europe did," *CNBC*. URL: https://www.cnbc.com/2019/06/07/how-google-facebook-amazon-and-apple-faced-eu-tech-antitrust-rules.html (Accessed: 20 September 2020).

Simes, Dimitri. 2020. "Russia up in arms over Chinese theft of military technology," *Nikkei Asia*. URL: https://asia.nikkei.com/Politics/International-relations/Russia-up-in-arms-over-Chinese-theft-of-military-technology (Accessed: 20 March 2021).

Strachan, Hew. 2005. *European Armies and the Conduct of War*. Routledge: London and New York.

Waltz, Kenneth. 1981. "The Spread of Nuclear Weapons: More May Better," *Adelphi Papers*, Number 171. London: International Institute for Strategic Studies.

# Technology and Society in Historical Context

**2**

**Abstract**

This chapter traces the long-term societal and political determinants in the history of technological development. Especially noted are the differences in prevalence of technological innovation across different societies, emphasising the particular roles of (domestic and international) political contingency and culture. The chapter explores insights on invention, necessity and innovation, as well as how less technologically developed societies can and have caught up with their more advanced counterparts — and why they sometimes do not. In summary, this chapter provides the necessary background and theoretical framework to the rest of the chapters that follow.

**Keywords**: 4IR; co-evolution of technologies; history of technology; innovation; invention vs necessity; Moore's law; Ratchet effect

## 2.1 Introduction

This chapter traces the societal determinants in the history of technological development. Especially noted are the differences in prevalence across different societies. The chapter explores the contemporary workings of this, as well as how less technologically developed societies can and have caught up with their more developed counterparts. We establish the relationship between necessity and invention. In so doing, this chapter provides the necessary theoretical framework and historical context for correctly understanding what gave rise to technology, its sustenance and ratchet in a manner that sufficiently gives background for the rest of the chapters to follow in this book.

Section 2.2 offers a historical account of the development of technology, underpinned by a brief case study of the origins and rise of Silicon Valley. Integral to this story is the role played by the international politics of its time, from WWII to the Cold War which followed and the incentives these events

17

put in place. Section 2.3 reviews the causal relationship between necessity and technological invention. Section 2.4 understands the current phase of this progression (i.e., the road to the 4IR). We conclude in Section 2.5 with an overview of the possible trajectories of AI in terms of different niches being apparently carved out by different countries per their published AI strategies.

## 2.2   Evolution of Technology from the Paleolithic to the Digital Age

Figure 2.1 captures an outline of key milestones in the history of *homo sapiens* and the evolution of technology that reflects the historical epochs within which we can locate the attainment of new stages of technological development.

Yuval Noah Harari in his classic *Sapiens* and follow-up *Homo Deus* covers some aspects of evolution of human beings to the present times where humans and machines are converging. Kenyan paleoanthropologist Richard Leakey (1984: 93–94) saw in the Upper Paleolithic period (occurring some 40,000 to 10,000 years ago) "evidence of the modern human mind at work," in contrast to earlier eras wherein "stasis dominated··· [with] change being measured in millennia rather than hundreds of millennia." Concurring with this, subsequent works have described the period as "the big bang of human culture," as it saw levels of innovation which outweighed the combined period of six million years that had come (Gabora and Russon, 2011: 7–9). The facets of this period that are regarded as most impressive are not the introduction of new artifacts, but the gradual, cumulative and sustained modifications to the appearance and functionality of pre-existing tools. This process is described as the "ratchet effect" which is found only among human groups (Tomasello, 2014; Gabora and Russon, 2011). With the end of the Ice Age (10,000 to 12,000 years ago), we see the beginnings of agriculture in the Middle East, as well as the invention of the wheel. Between 5,000 and 6,000 years ago, written languages developed in Eurasia, followed by mathematical calculations around 4,000 years ago. Philosophical works emerged 2,500 years ago in classical Greece, with the arrival of the printing press 1,000 years ago in China, during the medieval period (the so-called Dark Ages in European history). The Renaissance, starting in the late 1400s, saw advocacy for the scientific method 500 years ago under the active promotion of Francis Bacon (Gabora and Russon, 2011: 11). This greatly facilitated the emergence of the Scientific

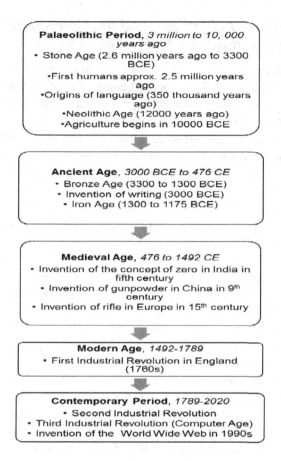

Fig. 2.1. Outline of historical timelines and technology.

Revolution, which saw, among others, the works of Isaac Newton which encapsulated the laws of motion. These in turn laid the foundation for the Industrial Revolution in England a century later. More recently, the past century has seen technologies disrupt traditional ways of life and reshape the daily lives of people, and by extension other living beings (Gabora and Russon, 2011: 12).

This technological change, especially in the past 500 years, did not occur in a historical and political vacuum. Indeed, it is integral to understand the set of international political events which led to the formation of the world's technological hub, Silicon Valley. Doing so requires insights from economic history, institutional economics and IR.

## 2.2.1 *International Politics and the Contingent Origins of Silicon Valley, 1890s to Present*

"In the early 20th century, Silicon Valley was just another stretch of California's rolling hill country." So observes Loeffler (2019). The town (officially called Santa Clara Valley) in California stretches about 25 miles, but contains technology parks and offices, whose economic productivity matches and exceeds even industrialised countries. For this reason it has become known as Silicon Valley[1] in homage to the electronics revolution it ushered in, making its name a byword for high levels of world class innovation, exemplified, above all, by its introduction of the Computer Age and being a contributor to the US's unparalleled wealth (Loeffler, 2019). In a nod to Silicon Valley's success, numerous countries have sought to emulate the Silicon Valley experiment, with a view to recreate what they see as the perfect technological ecosystem. But how did this region come about? A look at the origins and growth of Silicon Valley showcases the region's contingent origins, with World War II and the US–USSR competition which characterised the Cold War as major catalysts.

In the late 19th century (as late as the 1890s), the region was originally renowned for its agricultural produce of French plums, which were processed into prunes and then exported. The region accounted for some 30% of the global output of this fruit, in addition to other crops such as pears and apricots. An integral event in the history of Silicon Valley was the opening of Stanford University in 1891 from a substantial donation by railroad magnate and politician Leland Stanford. In turn, the university's crop of engineers would be taught and guided by Frederick Terman, who mentored many of those who went on to establish companies in the vicinity of the university and make Silicon Valley what it became. Indeed one of his central goals was ensuring that the region would no longer be as characterised by a brain drain as it was:

> "Considered by many as a founding father of Silicon Valley, Terman spent the following decade after joining the faculty building up the university's modest electrical engineering program into a top-tier one. This dedicated work became frustrating, however, as he watched the university produce highly-educated graduates, only to see them earn their degrees and leave town the

---

[1] Silicon being an element which is instrumental in manufacturing transistors.

following day for jobs with engineering firms on the east coast" (Loeffler, 2019).

Instead, he wanted to see Stanford alumni stay in Santa Clara Valley and establish enterprises that would in time create a sustained industry. In pursuit of this, he made use of his position to encourage Stanford graduates to remain in the region, instead of going east to find employment as had been the practice. Among the first to heed this call were the founders of Hewlett-Packard. William Hewlett and David Packard founded Hewlett-Packard in 1939 in Palo Alto at the insistence of Terman to form an electrical test equipment company. Terman's message started gaining traction as some graduates and even faculty members established their own aerospace and electronics ventures in the region. A strong academic curriculum backed this commercialisation and industrialisation activity, ensuring a steady supply of well-trained employees to work in the local enterprises. This is a pipeline that continues to this day. Although such industry-university collaboration is a feature common to many countries and college towns, what set Silicon Valley apart was the influx of funds from the government, particularly the US military, with the outbreak of WWII.

Silicon Valley set itself apart at this time as it was the only place that had the capacity to produce radios, headsets and radar systems at sufficient scale during the outbreak of the war. It was also advantaged by geography. With the US fighting not only in Europe against Germany and Italy but also against Japan, the west coast-based Silicon Valley (at a very short distance from the Port of San Francisco), availed itself as the most viable location for the production of the needed electronics, microwave, and radar equipment for the US Navy and Airforce in the Pacific. After the war, Stanford's fortunes continued to expand. In 1948, the university welcomed over a thousand new students who were former soldiers during the war, funded by the US government through the Government Issue Bill:

> "The large influx of government investment into the university through this program allowed the school to expand its facilities and the school of engineering that Terman had built up in his time as a faculty member was full of promising young students who had spent several formative years working hand-in-glove with the US military. When they graduated, they — along with engineering graduates from across the country — would form a corps of engineers the world had likely never seen before or since" (Loeffler, 2019).

The commercially relevant innovativeness of the region saw a boost with the work of the Nobel Prize laureate William Shockley and his staff, most prominently John Bardeen and Walter Brattain, who invented the point-contact transistor at AT&T's Bell Laboratory in New Jersey.

"With the backing of Fairchild Camera and Instrument in Long Island, NY, eight engineers from Shockley's lab resigned, including Gordon Moore and Robert Noyce, to form Fairchild Semiconductor in 1957 [in Silicon Valley]. Led by Noyce, Fairchild would eventually grow into the most important company in the history of the Santa Clara Valley after Noyce independently invented the Integrated Circuit" (Loeffler, 2019).

Shockley, Bardeen and Brattain went on to share the Nobel Prize in Physics for the invention of the transistor, while Bardeen received a second Nobel Prize for superconductivity. The integrated circuit has been called the key invention of the Computer Age, and in 1973 the editor of *Electronic News* referred to the region as "Silicon Valley" as a result of the magnitude of its silicon-based industries (Kenney, 2017). But world politics once again acted as a catalyst in the history of Silicon Valley. After the Soviet Union launched *Sputnik* in 1957, US legislators and policymakers realised that they could not predict the inventions that would become game-changers and thus "they would invest in all of them without prejudicing the expected outcome" (Loeffler, 2019). As a result, the government went on a funding spree, with the funds being available for all ideas: "With the national mood in a state of near hysteria in the years following *Sputnik*, Congress', as well as Presidents Eisenhower, Kennedy, Johnson, and Nixon's, only answer to Sputnik and the 'missile gap' was to throw money at anything that looked like it could be [a] promising technology that could give the US a leg up on the Soviets" (Loeffler, 2019). To a substantial degree, this bred and encouraged the risk-taking culture for which Silicon Valley is renowned and which made it a striking contrast to other, more cautious regions in the US and in the rest of the world where investors tend to be risk averse. This approach, based on a catch-all strategy that is based on invention and then necessity (elaborated on in the forthcoming section), led to some inventions that would not otherwise have been made. For example, the 1960s saw the Defense Advanced Research Projects Agency (DARPA) funding about 70% of all research into computational technologies globally. One of the agency's challenges was a call for the development of a computer system which would be impenetrable to Soviet attacks so that in the event of a USSR attack on a single university its work would be protected. This gave birth to ARPAnet, the precursor of the present-day Internet.

As mentioned earlier, the success of Silicon Valley has been inspirational to other governments around the world. The most successful case has been that of China's Zhongguancun, which boasts a GDP equivalence of US$437.6 billion (compared to Silicon Valley's US$275 billion). The Chinese region was envisioned by Chen Chunxian of the Chinese Academy of Sciences (CAS) after an official visit to Silicon Valley in the 1980s. Despite initial resistance to his vision and activities, the Chinese government eventually embraced the idea and poured funds into making Zhongguancun a high-tech center dominated by the private sector starting in 1983 according to the *Historical Dictionary of Science and Technology in Modern China* (Sullivan and Liu-Sullivan, 2015: 69). One of the major success stories from this is the Lenovo Group which, in 2005, bought IBM's PC division. Additionally, the region hosts many western companies' Asian headquarters including Intel, Oracle Corporation and Ericsson. These have a crucial research component that feeds into China's R&D.

## 2.3 Invention and Necessity: A Framework for Innovation

Jared Diamond — in asking whether all societies in a particular continent may be so unreceptive to a technology as to explain the generally slow rate of development — highlights the critical question of his 1997 opus *Guns, Germs and Steel*. Diamond begins by restating the common adage "necessity is the mother of invention" (1997: 242). In this regard, a litany of inventions do conform to this common sense view of "necessity-as-invention's-mother." For example, as the author recalls, in 1942, at the height of World War II, the United States government set up the Manhattan Project with the clear and stated goal of inventing a technology capable of building the atom bomb ahead of Nazi Germany (Diamond, 1997: 242). The project cost a contemporary US$2 billion (about US$20 billion in 2020 terms). Another is the 1794 invention of the cotton gin by Eli Whitney to replace the more laborious hand cleaning of cotton in the American South, a process which made slavery much more profitable than it had ever been before (Green, 1965). They would appear to vindicate the necessity-to-invention paradigm, but they are deceptions; they are exceptions rather than the rule.

"In fact, most inventions were developed by people driven by curiosity or by a love of tinkering, in the absence of any initial demand for the product they had in mind. Once a device had been invented, the inventor had to find an application for it. Only after it had been in use for a considerable time did consumers come to feel that they "needed" it. Still other devices, invented to solve one purpose, eventually found most of their use for other, unanticipated purposes" (Diamond, 1997: 243).

This leads to the notion of "inventions in search of a use," which rings true for most inventions; from airplanes, to automobiles, phonographs and transistors (Diamond, 1997: 243). The example of the phonograph is particularly noteworthy. After he had invented it in 1877, Thomas Edison published an article which suggested 10 uses for his invention. These uses include such applications as the recording of the last words of dying people, recording books for the blind, announcing clock times and teaching the alphabet. What was missing in Edison's list, however, was the application for which the phonograph would be put to the most use — recording and playing music. After some time, Edison even told his assistants that his invention had no commercial viability. When he did eventually change his mind on this, he sold them as office dictation devices and was soon scandalised to find out that his device had been used in jukeboxes. It took some two decades before the great inventor finally conceded, with some reluctance, that recording and playing music were the main uses of his phonograph.

The automobile is yet another example of an invention that was in search of a use. In 1866 Nikolaus Otto built his first gas engine. However, at the time, horses had been the main mode of transportation for 6,000 years and had only recently been supplemented by steam-powered railroads, with which all seemed satisfied: "there was no crisis in the availability of horses, no dissatisfaction with railroads" (Diamond, 1997: 243). Furthermore, Otto's invention was more than two meters tall and was weak and heavy. Only in 1885 did Gottfried Daimler "[get] around to installing one on a bicycle to create the first motorcycle; he waited until 1896 to build the first truck" (Diamond, 1997: 243). By 1905, there were motor vehicles in some use, but these were largely "unreliable toys for the rich" (Diamond, 1997: 243). It was to be some time before they proliferated to the near-ubiquitous status they have in modern industrialised and industrialising societies. Widespread public satisfaction with horses and rail was high until World War I when the militaries decided that they needed trucks upon which they received widespread adoption (Diamond, 1997: 243).[2] Society-wide use was not without prodding, however. There was a great deal of lobbying by the truck manufacturers to present the case for these new forms of transportation to the public so that they replaced horse-drawn wagons in industrialised societies.[3]

Thus, contrary to the common-sense view, "inventors often have to tinker for a long time in the absence of public demand, because early models perform too poorly to be useful" (Diamond, 1997: 244). This was the case with the first camera, the first typewriter and the first TV set. Indeed, this point is brought home by the recognition of the fact that while millions of patents are filed each year, only a few of them ultimately become commercialised. As the final section of this chapter briefly discusses, within the area of machine learning, it has been observed that patent authorities have relaxed some of the requirements for filing patents in order to widen the scope of intellectual property within their possession, with the aim of cordoning them off from use by other countries and with the hope that they can be developed (i.e., find necessity) at a later stage. Furthermore, even those inventions that do meet their purposes of design "may later prove more valuable at meeting unforeseen needs" (Diamond, 1997: 244). For example, James Watt's steam engine had originally been invented to pump water out of coal mines, and later found use in supplying power to cotton mills and then propelling locomotives and boats.

Thus, not only is the reverse necessity-invention paradigm unsound, it also overstates the importance of rare genius. The "heroic theory of invention" is encouraged by patent law, which requires proof of novelty and gives financial incentive for denigrating or ignoring previous work. Rarely, however, does Ms. X alone invent Widget A. Contrary to the simple narrative that, for example, James Watt invented the steam engine in 1769 after having been inspired by watching steam rise from a tea kettle's spout, there is

---

[2]This hints at a process of co-evolution which rendered the trucks necessary to meet the challenges brought on by changes in other facets of war by 1914–1919. This will be explored in later sections of this chapter, and the role of militaries in the evolution of technology are discussed in Chapter 6 and Chapter 8.
[3]This indicates a political-economy interaction that will be returned to later in the chapter and in greater depth in Chapter 4.

a much longer history of previous incremental inventors to whom he was a successor:

- Watt had gotten the idea for his particular steam engine while repairing a model of Thomas Newcomen's steam engine, already 57 years in existence and a commercial success.
- Newcomen's engine, in turn, was modelled along the steam engine of Thomas Savery which had been invented in 1698.
- That had itself followed the Frenchman Denis Papin's design from around 1680.
- This itself had been based on the ideas of the Dutch scientist Christiaan Huygens and others.

Similar to Watt's invention derived from pre-existing inventions, the Wright brothers' manned powered airplane came in the wake of the manned unpowered gliders of German 19th-century inventor Otto Lilienthal and the unmanned powered airplane of American astronomer Samuel Langley (Skrabec, 2006: 24). The latter reportedly unsuccessfully sought collaboration with the Wright brothers, but they later won the Smithsonian Institution award named after him (the Langley Gold Medal) in 1910 for "meritorious investigations in connection with the science of aerodynamics and its application to aviation" (Smithsonian Institution, 2018). Another future recipient was Robert H. Goddard, who demonstrated the first liquid fuel-powered rocket engine in 1926, which enabled space exploration to magnitudes even he could not have foreseen, given the impetus later given to space exploration by the Cold War in the form of the Space Race (1955–1975).

## 2.4  The Road to the Fourth Industrial Revolution

In recent literature on technology lifecycles,[4] one of the salient problems and deficiencies in studies has been the inability to know in advance the

---

[4]The notion of technology life cycles was first introduced by Little (1981). "Since then most studies on technology life cycle analysis have a firm [but error-prone] assumption that a technology or a group of technologies has a cycle of inception, growth, saturation and retirement. Following this assumption, scholars and practitioners have attempted to figure out an S-curved or double S-curved technology progression relationship to predict the future of that technology using past and present information" which Lee *et al.* (2017: 55–57) seek to modify by introducing a new methodology of "patent citation analysis to measure technology life cycles."

endpoint of any given technology's lifecycle since what can be measured with any level of accuracy are proxies that may have no direct link or predictive coherence. Lee *et al.* (2017) raise this point with particular regard to patent counts:

> "For example, one might ask, what is the current phase of a technology's progression when the patent application count is 100? Can we say that the technology has transitioned from one phase to another if the patent application count changes to 150? Or, is it just a fluctuation in the same phase?" (Lee *et al.*, 2017: 55).

So, the necessity-to-invention paradigm is not necessarily true. Nevertheless, societal context is still very important in the lifecycle of any technological invention as it determines the degree to which it will take root in the first place. As we have seen, inventors have had predecessors upon whose work they subsequently built and without whose prior work they might not have made their discoveries. The most historically recognised example of this invention-in-a-vacuum problem is that of the Phaistos Disk (in Fig. 2.2.) whose inventor anticipated the type print by 3,000 years but essentially created a device that could not be exploited at the time of its creation.

A related observation is made by Porter *et al.* in their 1986 article "New Form of Industrialization: Microcomputers in Developing Countries," which was an impact assessment of computer uptake in three distinct forms of

Ø = 16cm

Fig. 2.2. The Phaistos Disk, presumably created in Crete around the 2nd millennium B.C. *Source*: Creative Commons.

developing world societies;[5] they state that "the 'push' provided by the supply of powerful information technologies needs to be complemented by the 'pull' of a demanding market" (p. 326). Thus, "merely having a bigger, faster, more powerful device for doing something is no guarantee of ready acceptance" (Diamond, 1997: 247). But, what *does* promote an invention's acceptance by a society? Diamond suggests four key factors:

1. Relative economic advantage compared with existing technology.
2. Social value and prestige.
3. Compatibility with vested interests.[6]
4. Observability of advantages.

This begs another question: how do differences in receptivity among societies arise? Diamond cites 12 explanatory factors that have been proposed by historians of technology.[7] These fall into two broad categories; economic-organisational and ideological. The economic-organisational factors explicated in the following manner:

1. The availability of cheap slave labour in classical times supposedly discouraged innovation then,[8] whereas high wages or labour scarcity now stimulate the search for technological solutions.

---

[5]"They range from nations on a pre-industrial level (e.g. certain African countries concerned with agricultural production and public health) to those on a second, beginning industrialisation level (e.g., certain Latin American countries), and on to those on a third relatively advanced industrialisation level (e.g., certain Asian nations heavily involved with technological adoption and industrialisation operations)" (p. 322).

[6]For example, the QWERTY keyboard was designed in 1873 to slow down efficiency of typists; it was made to favour left-handed people because the majority of people are right-handed and were typing so fast that the original user friendly models would jam. When more efficient and non-jamming models were introduced in 1932, they were found to allow typists to type at twice their normal speed and without jamming. However, "vested interests of hundreds of millions of QWERTY typists, typing teachers, typewriter and computer salespeople and manufacturers have crushed all moves toward keyboard efficiency" (Diamond, 1997: 248).

[7]These are taken fully on board by Niall Ferguson in his 2012 book *Civilization: The West and the Rest* in which he details these as special "apps" that allowed the West to be able to lead in science and connects it to successful empire building.

[8]A contrast is also made by some scholars (e.g. Goldin and Frank, 1975: 299) between the merchant-dominated and enterprising American North which had no slaves and their Southern counterparts who did and were primarily agricultural and conservative.

2. Patents and other property laws reward innovation.
3. Modern industrial societies present extensive opportunities for technical training; as medieval Islam did and as the modern Central African Republic, for example, does not. In more contemporary parlance, these are referred to as technological ecosystems.
4. Modern capitalism, in contrast to the more ancient economies of the Roman empire for example, is organised to be more capable of rewarding those who invest in technological development.
5. The strong individualism of Western society allows successful inventors to keep earnings for themselves.

The ideological factors, on the other hand, include the following:

6. Risk-taking behaviour, which technology historians see as most effective in encouraging efforts when they are sufficiently widespread. Evidently, they are unevenly spread throughout different societies.
7. Historians also argue that the scientific outlook was a unique feature of post-Renaissance Europe, and in turn laid the foundations for its technological leadership.
8. In relation to the previous point, religions vary greatly in their relation to technological innovation. This point is emphasized in Max Weber's 1905 opus *The Protestant Ethic and the Spirit of Capitalism*.

The notion that intergenerationally learned behaviours and information (key pillars of culture) are distinct to humans is a widely held anthropological truism backed by many studies in comparative psychology (Tomasello, 2014). In his text, *A Natural History of Human Thinking* (2014), Max Planck Institute of Evolutionary Anthropology comparative psychologist Michael Tomasello brings decades of research on apes to argue that the emergent group-mindedness, unique to *homo sapiens*, among all members of the cultural group (including "in-group strangers") rests on an ability to construct common cultural ground through conventions, norms and institutions (2014: 15). Studying the link between culture and technology requires parsimonious definitions of both, in addition to an understanding of the potential lack of falsifiability. This is made apparent, for example, in Steers *et al.* (2008: 257) when they critique the notion sometimes implied in Western studies that seek to ask why some discoveries made in the West were not made in China or the Muslim world where the foundational insights for those technologies were initially made and then diffused to the West. Basalla (1998: 173) illustrates a key pitfall of this line of investigation: such studies make the assumption that the discovery in question would have been interpreted and adapted in a linear fashion in the same manner regardless of the cultural context.

Understanding culture (behaviourally) to mean the ways in which given societies solve their problems in distinction from other societies, Steers *et al.* (2008: 255) ask two important, interconnected questions: "To what extent can differences in national cultures systematically influence whether and for what reasons nations adopt — or fail to adopt — available emerging technologies?" Their cases of interest are Brazil and South Korea. On the former they are keen to know why, despite being ranked in the mid-30s for innovation, the country was able to become the first to affect the switch from petroleum to ethanol ahead of the US, the EU and Asian countries who appeared better poised to do so. Their paper advances possible explanations but identifies culture as the most salient. They propose the cultural outlook of *jeitinho* as being central in this regard. Literally, the term translates to *little way*, but more broadly it refers to "an innovative problem-solving strategy in which the individual uses social influence combined with cunning tricks to achieve goals, despite the fact that it breaks formal rules" (Rodrigues *et al.*, 2011: 29). In the case of South Korea, their issue of interest is the emergence of this country, regarded as a late industrialiser, to become the world leader in internet installation and speed by 2003. In this case, they highlight the identified role of the country's interpersonal network-oriented culture (a concept known as *in-maek*).

An additional four factors are given by Diamond, but these can variously support or inhibit technological development, and therefore, require typological thinking around their various configurations:

9. War: which can encourage innovation through increased R&D but can also result in downward pressure and disruption of industries which are mobilised for war efforts.
10. Centralised government: which can facilitate R&D expenditure but can just as well put in place policies which disincentivise the innovativeness which is nominally seen in laissez-faire societies.
11. Climate: as adaptation can yield innovative solutions but it may also result in shortages which stand in the way of completion of innovative implements.
12. Resource abundance: which can readily fulfil inputs but may disincentivise innovation through a process named the resource curse.

All twelve of these hypothesised variables, which have rarely been universally tested, are theoretically plausible. However, none of them are necessarily tied to geography and therefore cannot explain why some parts of the world are more innovative than others. Furthermore, there is variance in acceptance of new technologies in the same continents, including of Western technologies in latterly colonised societies. In a contribution to the 2014 volume *Africa's Development in Historical Perspective*, Clarence-Smith assessed textile factories in East Africa after independence and found that they soon reached a state of disrepair because they had no moorings with the societies they were in, who preferred to work in less industrially intensive methods (p. 287). On the other hand, the Asian experience was characterised by technological transfers and then internal innovation that has resulted in Japan, South Korea and Taiwan becoming some of the leading players in electronics manufacturing. Reflecting the variety of experience in the more managed processes of innovation with active government involvement (which in turn must be involved in a manner that is still able to make space for the private sector), the Asian case studies are characterised by top-down policies in terms of import and export controls, availing of investments, education but also tax incentives and industry support which took cues from private businesses in a bottom-up fashion. The latter was characterised by pragmatism towards failing companies, while also opening up for foreign manufacturers (Mills *et al.*, 2019). In turn, this paved the way for knowledge transfers and adaptation as the Asian companies carved their own niches in the electronics global value chain.

Noticeably, there are temporal differences in embraces of technology; the ancient Greeks and Romans were more accepting of innovation than their medieval successors who lived in the Dark Ages. The conventional wisdom is that useful technologies, by virtue of their utility, can never be lost and can only be replaced by better versions of themselves. However, there are many factors — many of them unpredictable — which determine the maintained use of a technology. Diamond cites the case of Japan, which in 1543 had discovered guns (brought by the Portuguese) and by 1600 had mastered and improved on them. However, they went back to the more prestigious sword, which was important to the samurai as a mark of distinction and work of art. The Japanese were not the only ones with such inclinations:

> "Contemporary European rulers also included some who despised guns and tried to restrict their availability. But such measures never got far in Europe, where any country that temporarily swore off firearms would be promptly overrun by gun-toting neighboring countries" (Diamond, 1997: 258).

China, a world leader in sea exploration between 1403–1433, intentionally closed down ship-building as a matter of policy. Without sufficient diffusion, fewer technologies stand to be acquired and existing technologies can be lost. This is made all the more important by the fact that technology builds on prior discoveries that have had a wide reach. The history of some technologies therefore demonstrates what is called the "autocatalytic process" which refers to the tendency of technology to speed up at a rate that grows over time because the process becomes its own catalyst (Diamond, 1997: 258). Nowadays, in the globalised context, the prospect of lost technologies is regarded as an improbability. Indeed, there has been no great technological reversal. Quite the opposite, in fact, has taken shape in what is called "Moore's law", as the number of transistors on integrated circuits doubles every 18 months to 2 years (Lambrechts *et al.*, 2018: 12). In some regards, even Moore's law proved too modest in 2014 when all the number of transistors installed in that year outperformed all previous installations ever made prior to 2011 (Theis and Wong, 2016: 41). Partially in recognition of this, we are regarded as being on the early stages of a 4IR.

In his book *The Fourth Industrial Revolution*, Klaus Schwab, founder and chairman of the World Economic Forum (WEF) notes that while the concept of an industrial revolution suggests "abrupt and radical change" it may not be considered singular, as events such as revolutions usually occur through a series of *incremental* innovations which propel economies and industries forward at a particular point in time (Schwab, 2016: 5). Nevertheless, novel technologies and perceiving them set off a profound transformation in economic and social systems (Schwab, 2016: 6). Cast in this way, since the 18th century, the world has undergone a series of industrial revolutions. The first, running from 1760 to 1840, started in Britain and was set in motion by the construction of the railroad and the invention of the steam engine and, in its wake, mechanical production (Trinder, 1982: 8). The second industrial revolution, ushered in during the 1870s to the early 1900s, brought about the possibility of mass production as it was characterised by electricity and the assembly line. The third industrial revolution, which began in the 1960s and culminated in the late 1990s, was defined by the computer/digital revolution. It was catalysed by the development of semiconductors, mainframe computers (invented in the 1960s), personal computers (invented and popularised in the 1970s and 1980s) and the Internet (invented in the 1990s by Tim Burners Lee).

The world is widely seen as standing on the cusp of the 4IR. This present revolution came at the behest of the digital revolution and is said to be defined by a more ubiquitous internet carried by smaller but more powerful sensors whose cost has decreased over time, as well as by machine learning-powered artificial intelligence (Schwab, 2016: 7). Already in their

2014 book *The Second Machine Age: Work, Progress, and Prosperity in a Time of Brilliant Technologies*, Andrew McAfee and Erik Brynjolfsson determined that the world is at an "inflection point" upon which automation will bring about unprecedented transformation in work and social relations. As they see it, the growth in computer dexterity makes it difficult to say what computers may be used for in the future. This is more so exacerbated by the interaction between the universally accessible Big Data to autonomous but interconnected computers and robots capable of AI, along with sensory devices which make possible the Internet of Things which will continue to form an even larger part of the ecosystem. These are thus the five trends which define the tilt towards the 4IR; physical (based on improvements in AI), 3D printing (also termed additive manufacturing), advanced robotics (characterised by the growing deployment of robots outside of factory settings), digital (characterised by sensors in the physical world connecting it to virtual networks), and biological (based on the growing ease with which the human genome is sequenced; with implications for biofuels, agriculture, sports and even organ development) (Schwab, 2016: 8–12; Marwala, 2020). Measurably, the 4IR will ostensibly be seen when these developments see mainstream usage. Importantly, however, societies are not on similar stages of attainment. This is perhaps most demonstrated by the fact that it is mainly the 30 industrialised OECD member countries and the European Union, along with the original BRIC and Kenya that have AI and cryptocurrency policies, with South Africa presently having a commission tasked with formulating a set of policies on the 4IR.

In retrospect, the scale of invention seen in the first industrial revolution seems impressive; however in medieval eyes the ingenuity displayed far outweighed that of the Bronze Age. In turn, this exceeded Upper Paleolithic ingenuity. Diamond argues that the rate at which a technology will be adopted is linked to the pre-existing technologies that complement it:

> "For instance, why did printing spread explosively in medieval Europe after Guttenberg printed his Bible in A.D. 1455, but not after that unknown Phaistos disk in 1700 B.C.? The explanation is at least partly that medieval European printers were able to combine six technological advances, most of which were unavailable to the maker of the Phaistos disk [paper, movable type, metallurgy, presses, ink and scripts]" (Diamond, 1997: 259).

This is substantiated by more recent studies as well. For example, Arthur and Polak (2006: 23) argue that technology evolves through the building of new devices and methods that build upon previously existing ones, "in turn offering these as possible components — building blocks — for the construction of further new devices and elements." In a follow-up book, Arthur (2009: 18–19) puts it more concretely, asserting that technologies emerge from combinations of pre-existing ones.

> "If you open up a jet engine (or aircraft gas turbine powerplant, to give it its professional name), you find components inside — compressors, turbines, combustion systems. If you open up other technologies that existed before it, you find some of the same components. Inside electrical power generating systems of the early twentieth century were turbines and combustion systems; inside industrial blower units of the same period were compressors. Technologies inherit parts from the technologies that preceded them, so putting such parts together — combining them — must have a great deal to do with how technologies come into being. This makes the abrupt appearance of radically novel technologies suddenly seem much less abrupt."

This argument has its origins in Schumpeter (1912), who famously observed that "to produce means to combine materials and forces within our reach," and that "to produce other things, or the same things by a different method, means to combine these materials and forces differently." This closes the explanatory gap left by theories that purely rely on the notion of eliminative processes whereby new, radically different and better technologies supposedly replace dominant ones. A newly proposed framework (Coccia and Watts, 2020) argues that "although the concept of competition is frequently used in diffusion and evolution of innovation, technological evolution is often not only a process of competition." Further borrowing from the evolutionary ecology of parasites and building on findings made from a computational agent-based model (ABM) along with historical data from four key technologies (passenger airplanes, farm tractors, freight locomotives and road racing bicycles), Mario Coccia and Joshua Watts (2020: 1) state that, in particular, technological parasitism gives a cogent explanation of the symbiotic relationship seen between "a host (or master) technology" and its "inter-related technologies." Their proposed mechanism has potential to explicate the relationships between technologies across markets in a way not hitherto done. In their findings, they show that:

> "[T]he passenger aircraft technology, a more complex technology with many parasitic technologies and a considerable level of interactions between associated systems and subsystems of technologies ... has the fastest rate of technological evolution. This empirical finding of faster evolution of technology associated

with a high number of parasitic technologies is also confirmed in the long run when aircraft technology is compared with bicycle technology" (Cocciaa and Watts, 2020: 9).

On the other hand, there can be what they term "a predator-prey relation," which is seen, for example, between a nascent technology and an established technology which is already in markets (Coccia and Watts, 2020: 3). In today's globalised world, the parasite-host model occurs on a wider scale. For example, Jérôme Galbrun and Kyoichi Jim Kijima's (2009: 195) study considered medical imaging technology in Europe and Japan between 1997–2008. Their findings show that medical companies clinically test technological alternatives and through this process clinical innovations which are not in the original patents emerge. In other words, technologies find new uses through deployment and use by geographically diverse communities of practice.

## 2.5  Conclusion: Towards 4IR Niches?

Artificial intelligence patents have been noticeably obtained in unprecedented scale than those in other traditional fields. Within China, AI patents are awarded for about 70% of applications across all fields, with that figure rising to more than 90% for the ML subset of AI (Okoshi, 2019). While indicative of a relaxation of criteria, it is also seen as part of the country's strategy as the Chinese government may be accepting as many patents on AI as possible to get ahead of other countries. This fits strikingly well with the Diamond-inspired paradigm of invention preceding necessity. The patents are being filed and accepted, sometimes without rigid proof of concept, due to the recognition by the authorities that they *may* become necessary at some future point. Machine learning patents may carry particular implications as they are technologies that will not only find future utility but will continuously learn and may accumulate the ability of inventing autonomously. A Massachusetts Institute of Technology study proposes that since they are trained on large databases, ML programs can explore all possible related molecules with potential health industry applications (Rotman, 2019). For this reason, Rotman predicts that the greatest impact of ML will not be in the applications we have so far imagined for it, but in its ability to imagine new areas of utility, that is "its ability to come up with new ideas to fuel innovation itself." This takes place against a background of observation by some economists, including a 2017 National Bureau of Economic

Research (NBER) study, that we may be running out of ideas despite growth in funding.[9]

Importantly (as is explored in the next chapter), this does not take place in a vacuum. Rather, it is taking place in a global environment characterised by differences in niches vis-à-vis innovation. Given the earlier noted and well demonstrated differentiations in innovation (which subsequently require diffusion), are we set to see a world in which different states lead in different aspects of AI? Analyses of published governmental strategies seem to imply this. While China's July 2017 AI strategy document (titled the "New Generation Artificial Intelligence Development Plan") was the most publicised and closely-watched (coming against the dramatic backdrop of the defeat of the Chinese Go champion Ke Jie by Google's DeepMind), over the 2017/2018 period, China was not the only country to issue an AI strategy.

Other countries include Canada (incidentally the first country to do so in early 2017), Denmark, the EU Commission, Finland, France, India, Italy, Japan (the second country to do so), Mexico, Singapore, South Korea, Sweden, Taiwan, the UAE, and the UK published theirs as well. It is against this backdrop that Dutton (2018) observes that "no two strategies are alike, with each focusing on different aspects of AI policy." Different strategies variously focus on scientific research (Canada, the EU Commission, and Mexico), talent development (Canada, Finland, France, New Zealand, South Korea and Taiwan), skills and education (Australia, Denmark, Finland, Poland, Singapore, South Korea and the United Kingdom), public and private sector adoption (China, Germany, Italy, New Zealand, Poland, Russia, South Korea, Sweden, the United Arab Emirates, the United Kingdom and the United States), ethics and inclusion (China, the EU Commission, India, Italy, Kenya, Mexico, New Zealand, Singapore, Sweden and the United Kingdom), standards and regulations (China, the EU Commission and the United States), and data and digital infrastructure (France, Japan, Kenya, Malaysia, Mexico, Singapore, Taiwan, the United Kingdom and the United States). Chapter 3 of this book establishes, however, that only a handful of countries are at the forefront of AI development, while Chapters 4 and 5 explore the competitive outcomes of this inequality (including the possible

---

[9]In their study 'Are Ideas Getting Harder to Find?,' Nicholas Bloom, Charles I. Jones, John Van Reenen, and Michael Webb find that "across a broad range of case studies at various levels of (dis)aggregation, we find that ideas — and in particular the exponential growth they imply — are getting harder and harder to find. Exponential growth results from the large increases in research effort that offset its declining productivity" (p. 1).

and actual military dynamics in the case of Chapter 6). Chapters 7 and 8, on the other hand, respectively examine the cooperative possibilities (and necessities) emanating from this in the form of regional integration and science diplomacy.

# References

Arthur, Brian W. and Polak, Wolfgang. 2006. "The evolution of technology within a simple computer model," *Complexity*, 11(5), 23–31.

Arthur, W. Brian. 2009. *The Nature of Technology: What it is and How it Evolves.* London: Penguin Books.

Basalla, G. 1998. *The Evolution of Technology.* Cambridge, UK: Cambridge University Press.

Brynjolfsson, Erik and McAfee, Andrew. 2014. *The Second Machine Age.* London: WW Norton & Co.

Clarence-Smith, William G. 2014. "Textile Industry of Eastern Africa in the Longue Durée" in Emmanuel Akyaempong, Robert H. Bates, Nathan Nunn and James A. Robinson (Eds.), *Africa's Development in Historical Perspective*, (pp. 264–294). New York: Cambridge University Press.

Coccia, Mario and Watts, Joshua. 2020. "A theory of the evolution of technology: Technological parasitism and the implications for innovation magement," *Journal of Engineering and Technology Management*, 55(1), 1–18.

Diamond, Jared. 1997. *Guns, Germs and Steel.* New York: Vintage Books.

Dutton, Tim. 2018 (June 28). "An Overview of National AI Strategies," *Medium.* https://medium.com/politics-ai/an-overview-of-national-ai-strategies-2a70ec6edfd (Accessed: 20 March 2021).

Ferguson, Niall. 2012. *Civilization: The West and the Rest.* New York: Penguin.

Gabora, L. and Russon, A. 2011. "The Evolution of Human Intelligence," in R. Sternberg and S. Kaufman (Eds.), *The Cambridge Handbook of Intelligence*, (pp. 328–350). Cambridge UK: Cambridge University Press.

Galbrun, Jérôme and Kijima, Kyoichi Jim. 2009. "A co-evolutionary perspective in medical technology: Clinical innovation systems in Europe and in Japan," *Asian Journal of Technology Innovation*, 17(2), 195–216.

Goldin, Claudia D. and Frank D. Lewis. 1975. "The economic cost of the American Civil War: Estimates and implications," *Journal of Economic History*, 35(2), 299–326.

Green, Constance M. 1965. *Eli Whitney and the Birth of American Technology.* Reading, MA: Addison Wesley Educational Publishers.

Kenney, Martin. 2017. "Explaining the Growth and Globalization of Silicon Valley: The Past and Today," Berkeley Roundtable on the International Economy. URL: https://brie.berkeley.edu/sites/default/files/brie-working-paper-2017-1.pdf (Accessed: 29 September 2020).

Lambrechts, Wynand and Saurabh Sinha, Jassem Ahmed Abdallah, and Jaco Prinsloo. 2018. *Extending Moore's Law through Advanced Semiconductor Design and Processing Techniques.* Boca Raton, FL: CRC Press.

Leakey, R. 1984. *The Origins of Humankind.* New York: Science Masters Basic Books.

Lee, Changyong, Kim, Juram, Noh, Meansun Woo, Han-Gyun, and Gang, Kwang-wook. 2017. "Patterns of technology life cycles: Stochastic analysis based on patent citations," *Technology Analysis & Strategic Management*, 29(1), 53–67.

Loeffler, John. 2019 (August 2019). "The Origin Story of Silicon Valley — and Why We Shouldn't Try to Recreate It," *Interesting Engineering.* URL: https://interestingengineering.com/the-origin-story-of-silicon-valleyand-why-we-shouldnt-try-to-recreate-it (Accessed: 29 September 2020).

Marwala, Tshilidzi. 2020. *Closing the Gap: The Fourth Industrial Revolution in Africa.* Johannesburg: Macmillan.

Mills, Greg, Obasanjo, Olusegon, Desalegn, Hailemariam, and van der Merwe, Emily. 2019. *The Asian Aspiration: Why and How Africa Should Emulate Asia.* Johannesburg: Picador Africa.

Okoshi, Yuki. 2019 (March 10). "China overtakes US in AI patent rankings," *Nikkei Asia.* URL: https://asia.nikkei.com/Business/Business-trends/China-overtakes-US-in-AI-patent-rankings (Accessed: 20 March 2021).

Porter, Alan L., Rossini, Frederick A., and Shi, Hengde. 1986. "A New Form of Industrialization: Microcomputers in Developing Countries," *Impact Assessment*, 4(3–4), 321–335.

Rodrigues, Ronaldo Pilati, Milfont, Taciano L., Ferreira, Maria Cristina, Porto, Juliana B., and Fischer, Ronald. 2011. "Brazilian jeitinho: Understanding and explaining an indigenous psychological construct," *Revista Interamericana de Psicología/Interamerican Journal of Psychology*, 45(1), 29–38.

Schumpeter, Joseph. 1912. *Theory of Economic Development.* Cambridge, MA: Harvard University Press.

Skrabec, Quentin R. Jr. 2006. *The Metallurgic Age: The Victorian Flowering of Invention and Industrial Science.* Jefferson, N.C.: MacFarland & Company.

Smithsonian Institution. 2018. "Langley Gold Medal," Smithsonian Institution. URL: https://www.si.edu/newsdesk/factsheets/langley-gold-medal (Accessed 20 March 2021).

Schwab, Klaus. 2016. *The Fourth Industrial Revolution.* New York: Penguin.

Steers, Richard M., Meyer, Alan D., and Sanchez-Runde, Carlos J. 2008. "National Culture and the Adoption of New Technologies," *Journal of World Business* 43(1), 255–260.

Sullivan, Lawrence and Liu-Sullivan, Nancy Y. 2015. *Historical Dictionary of Science and Technology in Modern China.* London: Rowman & Littlefield.

Theis, Thomas N. and Wong, H. S. Philip. 2016. "The End of Moore's Law: A New Beginning for Information Technology," *Computing in Science & Engineering*, 41–50. URL: https://e3s-center.berkeley.edu/wp-content/uploads/2019/06/2017_The-End-of-Moore%E2%80%99s-Law-A-New-Beginning-for-Information-Technology.pdf (Accessed: 5 January 2020).

Tomasello, Michael. 2014. *A Natural History of Human Thinking.* Cambridge, MA: Harvard University Press.

Trinder, Barrie. 1982. *The Making of the Industrial Landscape.* London: History Press.

# Technology Flows and Transfers

# 3

**Abstract**

This chapter examines insights and debates on technology transfer from developed to developing countries. First demonstrating the glaring gap between the developing and industrialised countries in both production and consumption of commercial and even open source software (with its apparent low barrier to entry) through value chain analysis, it subsequently showcases the politics of transfers when there are military considerations at play. It proceeds to discuss how trade and Foreign Direct Investment (FDI) interact with the domestic setting of various countries in facilitating such technology transfers and concludes with a discussion on the changing nature of technology transfers in the era of AI and other emerging technologies.

**Keywords**: Absorptive capacity; FDI; global value chains; late developers; open source software; technology spillovers; technology transfer; trade

## 3.1  Introduction

An indicator of economic development, technological advancement can also be its antecedent (Lee and Tan, 2006; Zhang *et al.*, 2009; Liu *et al.*, 2016; Osano and Koine, 2016). Inequality within countries, due to the advent of mass automation, is among the most anticipated and therefore closely studied aspects of the 4IR. Literature studying economic inequality between countries as a result of this transformation is less prevalent, however.

The first three industrial revolutions determined present-day inequalities among countries. Eight of the ten largest technology companies in the world (measured by their market value and market share of their respective sectors) are American, including Apple, Microsoft, Alphabet (the parent organization of Google), Intel, IBM, Facebook, Cisco and Oracle. The other two, Samsung Electronics and Tencent Holdings, are South Korean and Chinese, respectively. Thus, some countries have a higher share of the tech sphere than others and appear poised therefore to play a bigger role in the 4IR. Indeed, in many regards they are leading it. Scholars, research groups, governments and international institutions such as the United Nations (UN), the World Bank and the World Economic Forum (WEF) have developed studies and initiatives on technology transfers from developed and industrialised countries to the less developed and industrialising countries. Through structures such as United Nations Conference on Trade and Development (UNCTAD), the UN has sought to actively catalyse this process of closing the gap. In its Sustainable Development Goals (SDGs) 9 and 17, the organisation elevates the significance of assisting late developers in innovation through partnerships. These works have variously identified trade and FDI as critical to the process of successful technology transfer to differing magnitudes. Proponents note that the transfer of technologies from developed to developing countries stands to be of benefit to the latter as they forgo the expensiveness associated with development and commercialisation of new innovations (Gerschenkron, 1962). Additionally, they are better positioned to learn from the errors of the pioneering and early adopter countries, especially around environmental sustainability (Hermosilla and Martínez, 2003: 1). In light of the Intellectual Property (IP) risks and security relevance of many technologies, developed country multinational corporations (MNCs) and governments have always sought to mitigate the unwanted transfer of sensitive technologies. This was especially the case during the Cold War. In more recent times, there have been contentions not only between the US, its allies and China, but also between China and Russia. This ranges from such far-flung areas as the provision of 5G infrastructure, fighter jets, mobile applications to social networks. The ostensible fears range from backchannels to reverse engineering. Given their integration to consumer culture, governance and security, the seemingly politicised nature of these value chains and sudden interruptions in flows have given substantial evidence for scholars working on the emerging area of "weaponised interdependence".[1] This is also indicative of a world undergoing major shifts

---

[1] See Farrell, Henry and Newman, Abraham L. 2019. "Weaponized Interdependence: How Global Economic Networks Shape State Coercion," *International Security*, 44(1), 42–79.

in the nature of the global value chain — the emergence of China in particular is indicative of what can be achieved by formerly backward countries.

A critical insight from the literature on technology transfers, and one which runs throughout all the seminal works and recent studies, is the necessity of an internal ecosystem capable of absorbing the foreign technologies into local contexts if it is to be successful. As the authors of an interdisciplinary and cross-country analysis — *How Nations Learn* — observe, "the ever-changing global economic, social, and political landscape of the twenty-first century has made technological learning and catch-up increasingly complex, particularly for nations that are latecomers to industrialization and structural transformation" (Oqubay and Ohno, 2019: 1). Indeed, what gave impetus to this multi-country study book was the recognition that not only is there unevenness in the world but that it also persists in the different capacities of various countries to realistically close the gap. Thus, while East Asian countries successfully conducted "catch-up," their Southeast Asian neighbours such as Malaysia, Thailand and Indonesia appear to be trapped in the middle-income trap, while countries on the African continent appear stuck in a "low-income trap" (Oqubay and Ohno, 2019: 2).

Section 3.2 briefly characterises the nature of the global technology value chain, and in so doing applies the framework to the software market, closing with a brief review of the emerging component of machine learning as well as the disruptions being brought to bear by cloud computing. This section also delves into the apparent inequality in the production of algorithms and application software, including in commercialised and non-commercial open source software. Section 3.3 offers an overview of the tools used for the measurement of such technological inequality and notes their differential geographical distributions. This provides a picture of the global landscape and leads to Section 3.4, which reviews insights and debates into the possibility and paths of technology transfer. Section 3.5 concludes the chapter with an evaluation of the resultant transformation in the nature of technology transfers at the behest of the 4IR.

## 3.2 The Technology Value Chain

In 1980, as part of a television series (and later a book) titled *Free to Choose*, economist Milton Friedman described the essentials of the global value chain (GVC) using a common and simple enough object, the lead pencil:

> "The wood from which it is made, for all I know, comes from a tree that was cut down in the state of Washington. To cut down that tree, it took a saw. To make the saw, it took steel. To make steel, it took iron ore. This black center — we call it lead but it's really graphite, compressed graphite — I'm not sure where it comes from, but I think it comes from some mines in South America. This red top up here, this eraser, a bit of rubber, probably comes from Malaya, where the rubber tree isn't even native! It was imported from South America by some businessmen with the help of the British government. This brass ferrule? I haven't the slightest idea where it came from. Or the yellow paint! Or the paint that made the black lines. Or the glue that holds it together" (Friedman, 1980).

The economist distilled the essence of the GVC as bringing together thousands of people from different cultures, around the world, who would indeed despise one another if they met, into a common task. "When you go down to the store and buy this pencil, you are in effect trading a few minutes of your time for a few seconds of the time of all those thousands of people" he observed (Friedman, 1980). The value chain is based on breaking down (or disaggregating) a firm's production into multiple components. Introduced by Michael Porter (1985), the value chain concept was originally aimed at understanding the competitive advantage of companies (indeed his book was titled *Competitive Advantage: Creating and Sustaining Superior Performance*). As Porter puts it,

> "The basic tool for diagnosing competitive advantage and finding ways to enhance [competitive advantage] is the value chain, which divides a firm into the discrete activities it performs in designing, producing, marketing, and distributing its product" (1985: 26).

Porter's value chain is defined by five primary activities (see 1985: 26) consisting of:

(1) inbound logistics,
(2) operations,
(3) outbound logistics,
(4) marketing and sales, and
(5) service.

Through segmentation of firms into various activities, the GVC generates an understanding of costs and sources of differentiation that can set a firm apart from competitors. This concept has also been found to be applicable to whole industries (Pussep *et al.*, 2011: 1) through applying the analysis to an abstract "typical" firm which is taken as a proxy for the entire industry since it would contain all, or a sufficient number, of activities typically seen in that industry. This approach, they argue, is particularly useful since we have seen growing levels of integration that has led to more competition between networks instead of firms.

The main types of global value chains include (1) market, (2) relational and modal, (3) captive/quasi-hierarchical and (4) hierarchical. The first describes those which see no direct interaction between the firms along the value chains working on the same product. The second describes that which exhibit cooperation between the lead firm and their supplier firms. In this regard, the supplier firms operate independently and may participate in joint planning sessions with the lead firms within the confines of the relevant governance and regulatory frameworks. The third kind, captive global value chains, are those which are made distinct by the asymmetrical relationship between the lead firms and the suppliers in which the former have the ability to monitor the latter. This indicates that the suppliers tend to be smaller and require support from the lead firms. This is most common in agricultural chains. The final sort, hierarchical global value chains, are characterised by fully internalised operations in vertically integrated firms. In technology, production tends to be characterised by hierarchical global value chains. In the post-WWII period, this has seen Western-designed and Western-owned technologies being manufactured in East Asian countries and marketed in neighbouring countries as well as globally. Sturgeon and Kawakami (2011) argue that firms such as Apple can maximise profit through value chains of this sort, and as a result they initiate or lead activities along the chain and tend to lean in favour of those asymmetrical relationships which can allow them market power while also outsourcing activities which are not core. From this perspective, the owning firms have tended to be headquartered in the US and Japan and have more recently become headquartered in Taiwan, China and South Korea.

Technologies in general are produced along GVCs. This means that they are the outcome of an international production process, by which materials are transformed based on designs and then marketed and sold out of a process which sees inputs made by people and organisations located globally. For example, the global software market, which boasted a total revenue of $347.8 billion in 2019 (equaling an annual growth rate of 2.4% per year between 2013 and 2017), most scholars conceptualize as having the following specific value chain nodes: the requirements value chain and the supply value chain. The former comprises four activities: (1) analysis and design, (2) implementation, (3) provisioning and (4) operation. The latter comprises the following activities: (1) implementation, (2) provisioning, (3) operation and (4) use.

Another distinction made by these scholars is a differentiation between application and infrastructure (being the industry's most profitable segment in 2019 at a total revenue of US$161.1 billion or 46.3% of total value). Some scholars argue that the use of software usually takes place in another industry, and thus "the value created should be attributed to the industry where the usage takes place" (Szyperski and Messerschmitt, 2003). Others break it down even further, identifying enterprise applications, enterprise mobility management, information management, security software and software infrastructure. In their paper Pussep *et al.* conceptualize a software specific value chain, by aggregating and unifying findings from a literature review of industry-level value chains in the software and related sectors as well as industry executive interviews. Their resulting unified software value chain comprises 11 activities: "product research, component procurement, product development, user documentation, production and packaging, marketing, implementation, training and certification, maintenance and support, operations, and replacement" (Pussep *et al.*, 2011: 1). This is somewhat akin to the ML value chain which consists of the following steps: (1) Data collection; (2) Data storage; (3) Data preparation; (4) Algorithm training; and (5) Application development. These stages involve (1) obtaining raw data; (2) placing raw data in data centers; (3) conversion, formatting and labelling of these raw data; (4) configuring an algorithm that can make predictions based on the data; and (5) converting these algorithmic predictions into commercial products and applications such as software with installations in mobile apps, medical diagnostic tools, military equipment, geospatial observation and self-driving automobiles among others.

Many valuable niche areas in the software industry are dominated by specialised service providers, and while many enterprises can and do self-publish their software (owing to their scale), a great many of them also seek to use other carriers for some niche segments of the market.

Globally, substantial portions of the market are affected by segmenting of applications which is being disrupted by cloud computing as it has migrated many functions to the Internet, highlighting the changes brought on by Big Data. This is set to continue to be the case due to the disruptive nature of the 4IR technologies. Effectively, "there is nothing to resell, technically install and there are no opportunities for providing any kind of logistics anymore" (Nieuwenhuis *et al.*, 2017: 3).

Despite comprising 17% of the planet's population and having the fastest-growing rate of mobile subscriptions, in 2019 Africa represented only 3% of the world's mobile app developers (compared to 29.7% and 29.4% for Europe and North America). Nevertheless, the presence of China, India and Singapore in lists of leaders in data centres is encouraging as they are countries which had been on the back foot during the inception of the first three industrial revolutions but have since become technology leaders in time for the fourth. Present-day Asia-Pacific represents some 34.4% of the world's software developers. Looking at some 2,650 open source software (OSS) projects developed in 20 different countries on GitHub, Mombach *et al.* (2018: 1) find that the number of projects in a country correlates to its GDP (with a Spearman's $\rho$ of 0.75). Thus even an area with an appearance of a low barrier to entry appears to be intricately tied to economic size. Incidentally, the United States was shown to have the largest number of projects (at 2,302 projects or 42% of the studied set), placing US contribution to global OSS code about three times higher than the second-ranking contributor, the PRC. These are in turn followed by the UK and Germany with no discernable contribution from Africa, Central America, the Caribbean and the Middle East. This demonstrates a high level of global inequality.

## 3.3 Technological Inequality

Technological inequality has been noted and tracked each year by the World Economic Forum since 2004 in its Global Competitiveness Index (and more recently the Global Competitiveness Index 4.0 since 2018). The reports seek to pin down the determinants of economic growth to a set of 12 pillars. These include the following: (1) Institutions, (2) Infrastructure, (3) Macroeconomic environment, (4) Health and primary education, (5) Higher education and training, (6) Goods market efficiency, (7) Labour market efficiency, (8) Financial market development, (9) Technological readiness, (10) Market size, (11) Business sophistication and (12) Innovation. Infrastructure (the subject of Chapter 5 in this book) is taken by the WEF to refer to effective modes of transport such as roads, railroads, ports and air transport and are regarded as mandatory for the success of any economy as they will facilitate businesses in getting their goods and services to consumers in a secure and time-efficient manner, while also facilitating the movement of workers to places of employment. Moreover, modern economies rely heavily on electricity which is insulated from constant interruptions to ensure continuous business and factory productivity. Finally, far-reaching telecommunications networks give rise to rapid flow of information which, as the WEF argues, improves overall economic efficiency through ensuring that companies can easily communicate and decide based on reliable and relevant information (Schwab, 2014: 6).

The WEF also takes stock of health and primary education among the population, stemming from the recognition that the health of a workforce is critical to any country's ability to compete and be productive. Recognising the continued relevance and centrality of humans to economies even in the 4IR, it argues that ill workers are not able to function to their potential and are less productive as a result. In turn, the ill-health of workers correlates with increased costs to businesses. This may be transformed in a context that is less human-centric given the advances being made in automation in the path to the 4IR. One human-centred metric will likely remain unchanged, however; the level of education of the population. Thus, in addition to the health of the working population, this WEF pillar also considers the quantity and overall quality of the basic education available to and accessed by the population. Such access to education in turn not only determines the individual efficiency of workers, but also contributes to innovation processes which require collective inputs. Less educated workers, on the other hand, are a liability to the production processes as they can do little beyond manual tasks.

In a similar vein, the WEF pays attention to the state of higher education (HE) and training in different countries as well, noting that the current global landscape requires countries to have educated workers with more than basic level knowledge. This WEF pillar tracks secondary and tertiary enrollments and the quality of education in the opinion of business leaders in order to ensure skills-industry coherence. In the era of AI and other emerging technologies, this also speaks to a country's ability to participate as a producer and not merely as a consumer of foreign technologies. The index is also alert to continuous and on-the-job training. Upskilling will thus be crucial to retain human relevance in the changing economy. An analysis by Gleason (2018: 5) paints a rather dim picture so far:

> "[T]oday's HE was designed to meet the needs of past industrial revolutions with mass production powered by electricity. Those systems are not suited for the automation economy. Today's students (of all ages) are faced with major challenges in demographics, population (both growing and shrinking ones), global health, literacy, inequality, climate change, nuclear proliferation, and much more. As students today leave university, the 4IR world has significantly different demands on them than have previously existed."

Unevenness — and therefore varieties in competitiveness — can also be noted in the measure of what the index labels Goods Market Efficiency (GME), under the rationale that the best ecosystems for the exchange of goods are those that are characterised by minimal government intrusions on business activity. In this regard, competitiveness may be hindered by "distortionary or burdensome taxes" as well as "restrictive and discriminatory rules on foreign direct investment (FDI) — which limit foreign ownership — as well as on international trade" (Schwab, 2014: 6). Consistent with the theoretical foundation established from Diamond in Chapter 2 of this book, the WEF also notes in this regard that market efficiency depends to a great deal upon "demand conditions such as customer orientation and buyer sophistication for cultural or historical reasons, customers may be more demanding in some countries than in others. This can create an important competitive advantage, as it forces companies to be more innovative and customer-oriented and thus imposes the discipline necessary for efficiency to be achieved in the market" (Schwab, 2014: 6).

More directly for our purposes in this chapter, the WEF measures aspects of technological readiness and innovation and their unevenness globally. In terms of technological readiness, the index rests on vast empirical research which shows that trade openness is correlated with growth in technological readiness (Schwab, 2014: 8). In terms of innovation, the report considers two types of innovation: non-technological and technological knowledge. The former related to innovations which have a close coherence with know-how, skills and working conditions which are integrated into the culture of organisations. In terms of the latter, the report argues that even though a lot can be economically gained from other pillars in the index, these are defined by diminishing returns. On the other hand, technological break-throughs are to be historically relied upon for new frontiers in productivity in the form of the successive industrial revolutions which began in mid-18th-century England (Schwab, 2014: 8; Marwala, 2020). Technological innovation has come to be associated with inequality due to its unevenness globally. By the WEF's analysis, countries which are lower-ranked can go a long way in moving up the index through adoption of existing technologies and investments in R&D by both the public and private sectors (Schwab, 2014: 9).

While these indicators are measured separately from each other, the reports nonetheless acknowledge the inter-relation among them, positing for example that the process of innovation relies on a conducive environment which is produced by private and public actors and leadership. Specifically, this requires adequate investments in R&D, capable scientific research organisations, as well as high levels of collaboration across institutions. This must all be underlined by high levels of IP protections (Schwab, 2009: 7). Furthermore, innovation would scarcely take shape in economies with inefficient markets (6th, 7th, and 8th pillars) or without extensive and efficient infrastructure (2nd pillar). Per their most important indicator, countries are in turn categorised in a typology that factors in their respective stages of development with those countries that are at lower stages of development being labelled as "Factor-based economies," those in the middle being labelled "Efficiency-driven economies," and those who are at the forefront being labelled "Innovation-driven economies." This is illustrated in Fig. 3.1.

In so doing, the rankings give consideration to pillars based on an economy's stage of development. Some examples of countries in each category as of 2019 are listed in Table 3.1.

The WEF makes use of two criteria in allocating countries into their stages of development. The first is GDP per capita at market exchange rates, and the second is the level of resource dependency:

"This is measured by the share of exports of mineral goods in total exports (goods and services), and assumes that countries with more than 70 percent of their exports made up of mineral products (measured using a five-year average) are to a large extent factor driven. Countries that are resource driven and significantly wealthier than economies at the technological frontier are classified in the innovation-driven stage" (Schwab, 2014: 321).

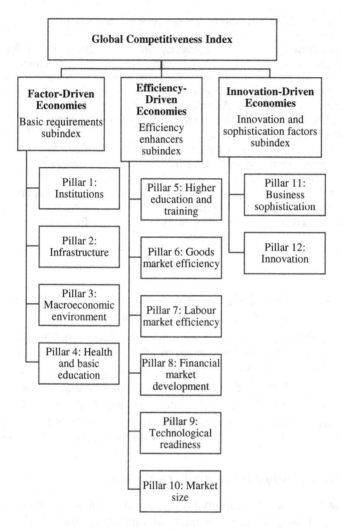

Fig. 3.1.   WEF typology of various economies by level of development.

*Source*: Adapted from World Economic Forum 2014–2015 Report (see Schwab, 2014: 9).

The typology takes into account ambiguity as "any countries falling between two of the three stages are considered to be 'in transition'. For these countries, the weights change smoothly as a country develops, reflecting the smooth transition from one stage of development to another" (Schwab, 2014: 321). The geographical distribution of the 35 factor-driven economies are represented on the map we generated in Fig. 3.2. A substantial majority

Table 3.1.    Summary of countries per typology.

| Factor-Driven Economies | Efficiency-Driven Economies | Innovation-Driven Economies |
| --- | --- | --- |
| Bangladesh | Albania | Australia |
| Benin | Armenia | Austria |
| Cambodia | Bosnia and Herzegovina | Bahrain |
| Cameroon | Brazil | Belgium |
| Chad | Bulgaria | Canada |
| Democratic Republic of Congo | Cape Verde | Cyprus |
| Côte d'Ivoire | China | Czech Republic |
| Ethiopia | Colombia | Denmark |
| The Gambia | Dominican Republic | Estonia |
| Ghana | Ecuador | Finland |

*Source*: WEF 2017/2018 Global Competitiveness Report.

of them are in Africa, with a few in Asia and one in the Caribbean (Haiti). Evidently, none are in Europe and North America.

On the other hand, two of the fifteen countries that were classified as being in transition from factor-driven to efficiency-driven economies were in Africa (Algeria and Botswana), while five were in the efficiency-driven category (Cape Verde, Egypt, South Africa, Swaziland and Tunisia). Overwhelmingly, as rendered on Fig. 3.3, none of those in the innovation-driven category were African. Technology transfers are one mechanism for development and movement up the index and the technological gap it implies.

## 3.4  Technology Flows and Transfers

Given the pre-existing economic and technological advantages of some nations over others (in some respects an outcome of the first three industrial revolutions [Shafaeddin, 1998; Inikori, 2002]), it can be observed that (with some notable exceptions) global capital is moving across these similar patterns as the world enters the 4IR, and in some regards thereby fortifying pre-existing economic parities. Technological readiness and innovativeness could be attraction factors for FDI, but FDI could also play a role in the presence and maintenance of these factors. Thus, countries which lack technological readiness and innovation-sophistication factors could be seeing less FDI because they lack these factors, whereas countries which have them could be experiencing the same or more FDI influxes because

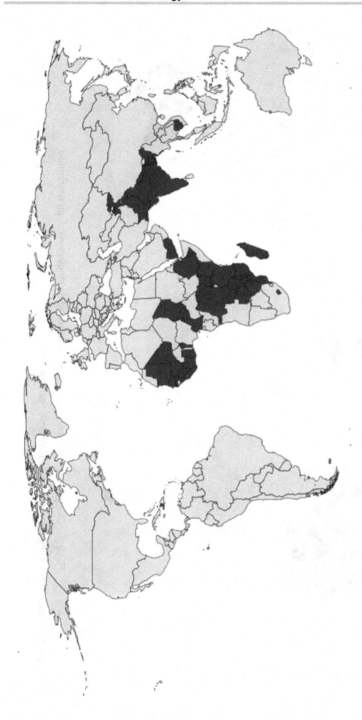

Fig. 3.2.  Countries classified as factor-driven economies.

Map by authors with data sourced from the World Economic Forum's 2017/18 report.

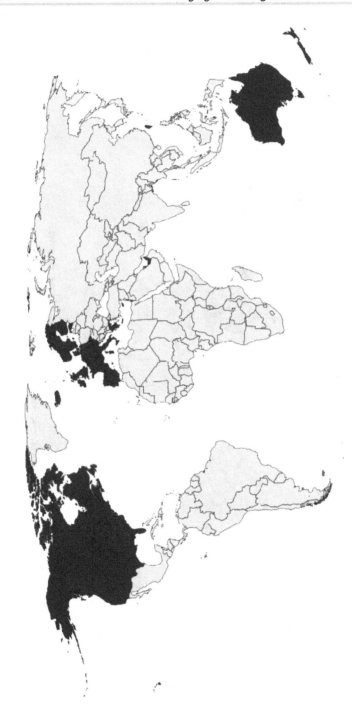

Fig. 3.3.   Geographical distribution of countries classified as innovation-driven economies.
Map by authors with data sourced from the World Economic Forum's 2017/2018 report.

they have technological readiness and innovation-sophistication in abundance. This raises the question of how possible it is for countries that are poorly positioned to take advantage of FDI and change their technological status from consumers to innovators. Given the state of globalisation, technological transfer is not only desired but inevitable to some extent.

In a global context in which technology is linked to military dominance, it may be observed that technology transfer is not an apolitical process. Nor is it a straightforward phenomenon. We study both aspects in this section, beginning with an assessment of the politics of emerging technologies during the Cold War, before turning to some of the complicated dynamics of technology transfer in more contemporary terms.

A recently declassified 1982 Central Intelligence Agency (CIA) report published observed that "Stopping the Soviets' extensive acquisition of military related Western technology — in ways that are both effective and appropriate in our open society — is one of the most complex and urgent issues facing the Free World today" (CIA, 1982: 1). The five reported methods of the Union of Soviet Socialist Republics (USSR) which the CIA identified include legal purchases of open technology, illegal purchases of controlled technology and clandestine activity, covert action by the Soviet intelligence community (e.g., the KGB and the State Committee for Science and Technology) who also influence "captured [US] scientists" (CIA, 1982: 5), actions by Soviet MNCs (who were also quasi state-owned), as well as recovered materials from the Vietnam War (hardware and data from downed planes which underwent reverse engineering). The report also notes that students and scientists participated in exchanges with the US or US-allied countries, with a concentration in the disciplines summarised in Table 3.2.

Notably, this is technology exchange among formal rivals and can be considered one form of technology transfer. Another is of the asymmetrical sort that takes place between developed and less developed societies. Various scholars have problematised and investigated the determinants of non-military technology transfer. In this regard, niches and advantages can be noted; whereas lead countries have the benefit of being more innovative and first movers, their less developed counterparts can adapt technologies developed by others. This gives a key advantage to economies of less developed countries (LDCs) due to the reduced cost of imitation and adapting technologies compared to creating them (as well as their markets, as discussed in Chapter 2; see Groizard, 2009: 1526; see also Gerschenkron, 1962). Academic literature has previously focused on imported capital since

Table 3.2.   The CIA's identified list of "Major Fields of Interest to Soviet and European Visitors to the United States".

| Computers | Architecture | Memories |
|---|---|---|
| | Automatic control | Numerically controlled units |
| | Computer-aided design | Networks |
| | Cybernetics | Pattern recognition |
| | Data bases | Programming |
| | Image processing design | Robots |
| | Image processing and retrieval | Software |
| Materials | Amorphous | Metallurgy |
| | Computer-aided design | Numerically controlled machine tools |
| | Composites | Powder metals |
| | Cryogenics | Superconductors |
| | Deformation | Testing |
| Semiconducters | Computer-aided design | Design |
| | Circuits | Ion implantation |
| | Defects | Production technology |
| | Devices | Surface acoustic wave devices |
| Communications, Navigation and Control | Antennas | Satellite communication |
| | Microwave/millimeter waves | Signal processing |
| | Radio wave propagation | Telecommunications |
| Vehicle/Transportation | Marine systems | Shipbuilding |
| Laser and Optics | Fiber optics | Optics |
| | Gas lasers | Tunable lasers |
| Nuclear Physics | Cryogenics | Reactors |
| | Fusion | Structural designs |
| | Materials | Superconductors |
| | Magnetohydrodynamics | |

*Source*: Central Intelligence Agency declassified report (1982).

it is likely to be technologically advanced and in so doing "contributes to higher productivity growth." At face value, this is the more straightforward manner of technological transfer since importing foreign technology consists of physical movement of technology products.

> "Multinational enterprises (MNEs) are seen as a vehicle of technology transfer. The literature also highlights that the transfer of technology might follow an internal transaction among parents

and affiliates, and similarly to the trade channel, either a transaction through markets with local firms or a spillover" (Groizard,
2009: 1528).

Proponents of this view also make the prescriptive claim that since many
of the materials required for technological products are sourced from the
developing world, they should be able to produce them more cost effectively
(Porter, 1990). There is a shortage of literature that proves this, however,
with countries such as Thailand and more recently China and India being
the exception rather than the rule and some products being more difficult to
produce than others in certain environments.[2] In fact, "there is evidence that
higher expropriation risk is associated with fewer and older technologies
transferred from parents to affiliates" (Javorcik, 2006) and that "lower quality
of intellectual property rights reduce the transfer from multinational parents"
(Branstetter *et al.*, 2006)." Nevertheless, cases of new start-up nations in
the form of Israel as well as Estonia[3] and Poland[4] among other former
Soviet satellites are proof that "latecomers" can still enter and in some
sectors lead the technology field. Recent evidence has indeed proved in
the main that trade is perhaps the most important and consistent pathway
for technologies to diffuse into developing countries from developed, as well
as among developed countries (Groizard, 2009: 1526–1527). However, the
variables which determine diffusion of technology do not always operate in a
linear fashion. For example, some studies show that effective IP protections
encourage trade while there is no clear demonstration that such protections
by themselves encourage technology imports universally. Other factors,
including human capital and domestic R&D have been identified as crucial
to encouraging technology diffusion (Groizard, 2009: 1527). Successive
studies have shown relative contributions of each (Silva *et al.*, 2019: 102;
Mazurkiewicz and Poteralska, 2017: 457).

---

[2]"However, it has been observed that global multinational companies (MNCs) establish R&D centres in China by means of alliances with universities and research
institutions or with local firm" (Liu *et al.*, 2012: 213).

[3]For example, Skype, among others, was founded in Estonia. The country also
boasts a near universal internet rate. When it gained independence from the Soviet
Union in 1991, its GDP per capita was US$3,044.38, by 2017 it was US$19,704.66.

[4]"In the last few years Poland has grown its tech and startup reputation, and is
now recognised as one of the most startup-friendly ecosystems across Europe and
beyond" (Trajkovska, 2019).

Various scholars have problematised and investigated the determinants of technology transfer. In his study, Griozard (2009: 1527) investigated the variables which determine technology imports over the period between 1970 and 1995 using a panel data of 80 countries. In the study, findings showed that domestic investments and FDI as well as the quality of IP rights lead to increased technological imports (Groizard, 2009: 1526). This demonstrates that countries without pre-existing financial means and technologies have a positively reinforcing circular flow; however, poorer countries can still take measures to increase their probabilities.

> "Results suggest that domestic and foreign investment positively influence high-tech imports. Moreover, importer countries may increase technology inflows improving the quality of IPR systems. We also find evidence that technology imports are associated with a large share of industry and a low share of agriculture in gross domestic product (GDP). Other factors exert a less robust role, such as trade openness or government expenditure. In contrast, countries with a human capital base strongly skewed towards unskilled workers import less technology from abroad. Finally, IPRs interact with FDI and human capital, suggesting that the role of FDI in fostering technology imports is higher the larger the protection of IPRs; the role of human capital reduces technology imports, the larger the protection of IPR" (Groizard, 2009: 1526).

The same author shows that there is some cross-country evidence showing that openness to trade is correlated with certain measures of technology adoption, such as changes in total factor productivity, larger investment in computers and rates of adoption of specific innovations (p. 1527–1528). As seen in Chapter 2, domestic demand and consumption are also key factors affecting the degree to which technologies will take root. There are, however, other means through which technologies move across borders. The most prominent is foreign direct investment. In recent years, African governments have also made it a condition of Chinese FDI that they be staffed by their citizens, along with commitments to skills transfers and/or personnel who possess knowledge of producing certain technologies.

In a seminal work, Teece (1976) demonstrated that the costs of technology transfer are substantial and decline with the age of the technology being transferred. The Yokota-Tomohara model argues that the degree of spillover varies depending on the interaction of industry and country characteristics with "skilled labor scarce countries [having] spillover effects only in low-tech industries, while skilled labor abundant countries have spillover effects in high-tech industries" (Yokota and Tomohara, 2010: 5). The magnitudes of technology spillovers are smaller for skilled labour scarce countries as compared to skilled labour abundant countries (Yokota and Tomohara, 2010: 5). How these conducive conditions are forged is the subject of the next chapter. But briefly, Cohen and Levinthal (1989) first put forward the concept of "technology absorptive capacity" when they study companies' R&D activities, and they argue that the effect of domestic R&D input on a corporation's technological progress has two aspects: (1) R&D output directly promotes the technological progress in the corporation and (2) domestic R&D input strengthens the host country companies' ability to imitate, learn and absorb the foreign technology, and helps them develop a stronger technology absorptive capacity to acquire more external technology spillovers. Xu *et al.* (2014) operationalise absorptive capacity as consisting of institutional change and human resource level. This becomes a factor in two basic points. Firstly, institutional change is regarded as the most far-reaching factor in economic activities as it sets the rules for the overall economy as well as in microeconomic terms. Secondly, the levels of human resource development, regarded as a "classical control variable," can be measured in terms of R&D investments whose outputs can be put to the test in terms of FDI and GDP growth at sub-national (i.e., state or provincial) levels to isolate for national trends.

## 3.5 Conclusion: The Changing Nature of Technology Transfer and FDI

Technological transfers have been undergoing critical analysis in recent literature. The Open Working Group on SDGs, for example, suggests an insistence on examining the impact of technology transfers beyond the mere attainment of new technologies by previously lagging societies and an emphasis on its equitable distribution within the societies. This aims to address both inter-state and intrastate inequality:

> "Assessment [of successful technology transfers] must be based on the application of the precautionary principle and founded on the need to involve various actors — particularly the intended users of a particular technology and those who will most likely be impacted — in decision-making across the technology development process" (Daño *et al.*, 2016: 5).

They further insist on evaluating new technologies through processes which are democratic, transparent and participatory as these will, they suggest, be essential to providing meaningful opportunities for receiving states and sections of their populations, including those in the margins (such as women), to participate in the deciding and evaluating the potential impacts of technology on issues which affect them — health, economic wellbeing, cultural heritage and the environment (Daño *et al.*, 2016: 5).

Increasingly, other parts of the world, in particular East Asia, are leaders in innovation. Traditionally, the region's story has been one of accelerated engagement with MNCs and acquisition of foreign technologies. In more recent times, we observe countries in the region join Japan in being characterised by the importance of their large domestic markets,[5] and by a shift towards design in addition to the production stage for which the region has been particularly noted. Since the early 2000s, Korean, Taiwanese and Chinese corporations such as Samsung, LG, Huawei, Xiaomi, Acer and HTC have become lead firms. The region also increasingly accounts for most of the new patents in the world. The PRC stands out:

> "Asia has strengthened its position as the region with the greatest activity in patent filings. Offices located in Asia received two-thirds (66.8%) of all applications filed worldwide in 2018 — a considerable increase from 50.8% in 2008 — primarily driven by growth in China. Offices located in North America accounted for just under one-fifth (19%) of the 2018 world total, while those in Europe accounted for just over one-tenth (10.9%). The combined share of offices located in Africa, Latin America and the Caribbean, and Oceania was 3.3%" (WIPO, 2019: 3).

Overall, of the countries in the global top five, three of the countries are Asian. In 2018, China (at 11.6%) and the Republic of Korea (at 2.5%) saw increases in the number of new patent applications; however, Japan (at −1.5%) registered a small decline (WIPO, 2019). On the other hand, India has also been "registering impressive increases" according to WIPO Director General Francis Gurry.

At the same time, other scholars have noted the changing nature of FDI with BRICS countries being both recipients and sources of new FDI in many countries to the same extent as traditional, Western financiers.

---

[5]Their governments, however, have become aware of their marginally decreasing population growths. This is especially true in Japan and China.

China's outward FDI (OFDI) grew from US$34.7 billion in 2001 to US$1.9 trillion by 2018. This represents a growth from 0.5% to 6.3% of global FDI stock in a space of less than 20 years (Schwarzenberg, 2019: 1). Indeed China's OFDI exceeded inward FDI for the first time in 2014 according to Ministry of Commerce of the People's Republic of China's calculations (García-Herrero, 2015; June 28), whereas firms in India make investments in a variety of sectors in different developing countries, though it is most concentrated in Singapore (Iqbal *et al.*, 2018: 98).

New technologies such as ML are also set to change how we conceive of the international hierarchy. A 2019 Carnegie Endowment report observes that no two countries are alike in their machine learning investment strategies. Overall, most fall into three broad categories: fast movers, moderate movers and slow starters. The first group consists of China and the United States and are set apart by their "heavily investing across most if not all nodes of the machine learning value chain." The second group, on the other hand, are defined by their focus on particular aspects of the value chain. Germany, Japan and Taiwan, for instance, are heavily investing in the physical capital required for data storage and algorithm training (like hyperscale data centers (HDCs) and supercomputers). Australia and South Korea are investing in the requisite intellectual capital (for example, R&D and STEM graduates). The third group are those countries which are yet to have clear strategies. Predictably, these are the developing countries who have neither the means of accelerated development nor the absorptive capacity of foreign technologies. Notable exceptions include Brazil, which entered the HDC market by capitalising on its cheap cost of energy, and Kenya, whose relatively high internet penetration rate could arguably enable significant data collection.

As a result of the sheer disruptiveness of the 4IR, countries on the lower end of the industrialisation indicators will have to shore up their science and technology diplomacy to facilitate technological transfer. Moreover, they will need to match these external efforts with increasing their absorptive capacity in the domestic sphere through appropriate policies. This is the subject of the next chapter.

# References

Arkebe, Oqubay and Ohno, Kenichi. 2019. *How Nations Learn*. Oxford: Oxford University Press.

Branstetter, Lee, Fisman, Raymond, and Foley, C. Fritz. 2006. "Do stronger intellectual property rights increase international technology transfer? Empirical evidence from US firm-level panel data," *Quarterly Journal of Economics*, 121(1), 321–349.

Central Intelligence Agency (CIA). 1982 (declassified 1999). *The Technology Acquisition Efforts of the Soviet Intelligence Services*. McLean, V.A.: Central Intelligence Agency.

Cohen, Wesley M. and Levinthal, Daniel A. 1989. "Innovation and Learning: The Two Faces of R&D," *The Economic Journal*, 99(397): 569–596.

Daño, Neth, Wetter, Kathy Jo, and Ribeiro, Silvia. 2016. "Addressing the "Technology Divides": Critical Issues in Technology and SDGs," Briefing Paper: Science, Technology and Innovation (STI) 6th Session of the Open Working Group on SDGs. URL: https://www.womensmajorgroup.org/wp-content/uploads/2016/07/WMG_6OWG_briefingPaper_Addressing_technology_divides_critical_issues_Neth_da%c3%b1o_Jo_wetter_silvia_ribeiro_2013_sus_dev_page.pdf (Accessed: 20 March 2021).

Friedman, Milton and Friedman, Rose. 1980. *Free to Choose: A Personal Statement*. New York: Harcourt.

Farrell, Henry and Newman, Abraham L. 2019. "Weaponized interdependence: How global economic networks shape state coercion," *International Security*, 44(1), 42–79.

Friedman, Milton and Friedman, Rose. 1980. *Free to Choose: A Personal Statement*. New York: Harcourt.

Gleason, Nancy W. 2018. "Introduction," pp. 1-11 in Nancy W. Gleason (Ed.) *Higher Education in the Era of the Fourth Industrial Revolution*. Singapore: Palgrave Macmillan.

García-Herrero, Alicia. 2015 (June 28). "China's outward foreign direct investment," Bruegel. URL: https://bruegel.org/2015/06/chinas-outward-foreign-direct-investment/ (Accessed: 4 December 2019).

Gerschenkron, Alexander. 1962. *Economic Backwardness in Historical Perspective: A Book of Essays*. Cambridge, MA: Belknap Press of Harvard University Press.

Groizard, José L. 2009. "Technology trade," *The Journal of Development Studies*, 45(9), 1526–1544.

Hermosilla, Javier Carrillo and Martínez, Pablo Chafla. 2003. "Technology Transfer and Sustainable Development in Emerging Economies: The Problem of Technology Lock-In," IE Working Paper WP 01/03. URL: https://econwpa.ub.uni-muenchen.de/econ-wp/othr/papers/0509/0509002.pdf (Accessed: 20 March 2021).

Inikori, Joseph E. 2002. *Africans and the Industrial Revolution in England: A Study in International Trade and Economic Development*. Cambridge: Cambridge University Press.

Iqbal, Badar Alam, Turay, Abdul, Hasan, Munir, and Yusuf, Nadia. 2018. "India's outward foreign direct investment: Emerging trends and issues," *Transnational Corporations Review*, 10(1), 98–107.

Javorcik, B. 2006. "Technological leadership and the choice of entry mode by foreign investors," in: B. Hoekman and B. Javorcik (Eds.) *Global Integration and Technology Transfer*. New York: Palgrave Macmillan and the World Bank.

Lee, Huay Huay, and Tan, Hui Boon. 2006. "Technology transfer, FDI and economic growth in the ASEAN region," *Journal of the Asia Pacific Economy*, 11(4), 394–410.

Liu, William Sheng, Agbola, Frank Wogbe, and Dzator, Janet Ama. 2016. "The impact of FDI spillover effects on total factor productivity in the Chinese electronic industry: A panel data analysis," *Journal of the Asia Pacific Economy*, 21(2), 217–234.

Marwala, Tshilidzi. 2020. *Closing the Gap: The Fourth Industrial Revolution in Africa*. Johannesburg: Macmillan.

Mazurkiewicz, Adam and Poteralska, Beata. 2017. "Technology transfer barriers and challenges faced by R&D organisations," *Procedia Engineering*, 182(1): 457–465.

Merton, R. 1968. "The Matthew effect in science: The reward and communication systems of science are considered," *Science*, 159(3810), 56–63.

Millington, A., Eberhardt, M. and Wilkinson, B. 2006. "Guanxi and supplier search mechanisms in China," *Human Relations*, 59(4): 505–531.

Mombach, Thaís, Valente, Marco Tulio, Chen, Cuiting, Bruntink, Magiel, and Pinto, Gustavo. 2018. "Open Source Development Around the World: A Comparative Study". URL: https://arxiv.org/pdf/1805.01342.pdf (Accessed: 11 October 2020).

Nieuwenhuis, Lambert J.M., Ehrenhard, Michel L., and Prause, Lars. 2017. "The shift to cloud computing: The impact of disruptive technology on the enterprise software business ecosystem," *Technological Forecasting and Social Change*, 129(1), 308–313.

Osano, Hezron M. and Koine, Pauline W. 2016. "Role of foreign direct investment on technology transfer and economic growth in Kenya: A case of the energy sector," *Journal of Innovation and Entrepreneurship*, 5(31), 1–25.

Porter, M.E. 1990. *The Competitive Advantage of Nations*. New York: The Free Press.

Porter, Michael E. 1985. *Competitive Advantage: Creating and Sustaining Superior Performance*. New York: The Free Press.

Prinsloo, Jaco, Sinha, Saurabh, and van Solms, Basie. 2019. "A review of Industry 4.0 manufacturing process security risks," *Applied Sciences*, 9, 1–31.

Pussep, Anton, Schief, Markus, Widjaja, Thomas, Buxmann, Peter, and Wolf, Christian M. 2011. "The Software Value Chain as an Analytical Framework for the Software Industry and Its Exemplary Application for Vertical Integration Measurement," *Proceedings of the Seventeenth Americas Conference on Information Systems, Detroit, Michigan August 4$^{th}$–7$^{th}$, 2011*.

Schwab, Klaus. 2009. *The Global Competitiveness Report 2008—2009*. Geneva, Switzerland: World Economic Forum.

Schwab, Klaus. 2014. *The Global Competitiveness Report 2013—2014*. Geneva, Switzerland: World Economic Forum.

Schulze, Elizabeth. 2019. "How a tiny country bordering Russia became one of the most tech-savvy societies in the world," CNBC. URL: https://www.cnbc.com/2019/02/08/how-estonia-became-a-digital-society.html (Accessed: 26 December 2019).

Shafaeddin, Mehdi. 1998. 'How Did Developed Countries Industrialize? The History of Trade and Industrial Policy: The Cases of Great Britain and the USA,' UNCTAD Discussion Paper No. 139.

Silva, Vander Luiz, Kovaleski, João Luiz, and Negri Pagani, Regina. 2019. "Technology transfer and human capital in the industrial 4.0 Scenario: A theoretical study," *Future Studies Research Journal Trends and Strategies*, 11(1), 102–122.

Sturgeon, Timothy J. and Kawakami, Momoko. 2011. "Global value chains in the electronics industry: characteristics, crisis, and upgrading opportunities for firms from developing countries," *International Journal of Technological Learning, Innovation and Development*, 4(1), 120–147.

Szyperski, Clemens and Messerschmitt, David. 2003. *Software Ecosystem: Understanding an Indispensable Technology and Industry.* Cambridge, M.A.: MIT Press.

Teece, D. J. 1976. *The Multinational Corporation and the Resource Cost of International Technology Transfer.* Cambridge, MA: Ballinger Publishing.

Trajkovska, Bojana. 2019 (January 28). "Warsaw's startup ecosystem at a glance," *EU Startup*. URL: https://www.eu-startups.com/2019/01/warsaws-startup-ecosystem-at-a-glance/ (Accessed: 26 December 2019).

Xu, Hao, Wan, Difang, and Sun, Ying. 2014. "Technology Spillovers of Foreign Direct Investment in Coastal Regions of East China: A Perspective on Technology Absorptive Capacity," *Emerging Markets Finance and Trade*, 50(1), 96–106.

Yokota, Kazuhiko and Tomohara, Akinori. 2010. "Modeling FDI-Induced Technology Spillovers," *The International Trade Journal*, 24(1), 5–34.

World Intellectual Property Organization. 2019. *World Intellectual Property Indicators 2019.* World Intellectual Property Organization. URL: https://www.wipo.int/edocs/pubdocs/en/wipo_pub_941_2019.pdf (Accessed: 4 December 2019).

Zhang, Yabin, Wu, Jiang, and Ai, Hongshan. 2009. "The technology gap and the limit of imitation: An inspection of the strategy of 'exchanging market for technology'," *Journal of Chinese Economic and Business Studies*, 7(4): 447–455.

# Policy, Politics and Emerging Technologies

# 4

**Abstract**

This chapter explores the policy factors which shape technological development within modern societies. In so doing, it explores in greater detail the relationship between domestic absorptive capacity and technology as well as examines the effects of emerging technologies on the domestic politics of various states, particularly in terms of state-society relations in democracies and non-democracies. We note the trends in the predictive role played by Big Data and the rise of blockchain. Importantly, the chapter observes the lowering of mobilisation costs brought on by these new technologies, while also rendering the democratic process vulnerable in new ways.

**Keywords**: Arab Spring, Blockchain; democracy and technology; innovation policy; R&D

## 4.1 Introduction

We have seen in the two preceding chapters how political factors shape technological development. The converse, that technological change shapes politics, is also true. Whereas the previous chapter looked into the policies that allow for meaningful adoption of foreign technologies, the present chapter looks into the domestic development of technologies.

Section 4.2 looks into the policy enablers of technological development within countries. It builds on literature which compares the different comparative advantages of countries. Importantly in this regard, there is no singularly successful innovation policy. Rather there is a litany of these. The section also explores the role of formal and informal institutions. Section 4.3 looks at the role of emerging technologies in changing the nature of political processes.

## 4.2  Policy Enablers of Technology

The process of developing a new industry — innovation — has been noted to be an especially risky process, replete with uncertainty over return on investment (Jiang and Zhang, 2018: 1). Writing in 1997 for the journal *Industry and Innovation*, David Soskice makes an important observation about one of the leading countries in terms of innovation. Germany, he argues, while lacking the market size of the US (272 million people) and even Japan (125 million people), has nonetheless been considered an extraordinary success in exports, and at even higher prices than average on account of the quality of its products. This, he notes, is due to Germany's capacity for innovation, which in turn is enabled by the institutional framework upon which German companies operate and are embedded within. As Soskice further explicates:

> "German patterns of innovation — incremental innovation in high quality products especially in engineering and chemicals — requires long-term capital, highly cooperative unions and powerful employer associations, effective vocational training systems and close long-term cooperation between companies and research institutes and university departments" (Soskice, 1997: 76).

He notes that the German incentives-constraints paradigm relies on these three basic conditions to achieve its hallmark model of incremental innovation and that in turn, the institutional arrangements (particular the role of powerful business associations) are able to resolve the problems of collective action and the shocks which may otherwise derail it. This, and the passing mention of the other two innovative economies of the 20th century (the US and Japan) should also shine light on Germany's idiosyncrasies, as well as the fact that each economy leverages many of its own idiosyncrasies. In many ways, then, there are as many configurations of innovation policies as there are innovative countries. Policymakers can put these in place in different countries. Thus, there is not only a dichotomy between effective and ineffective institutional arrangements for innovative success, but there also persist many correct institutional frameworks for encouraging innovation. As the same author puts it, "the underlying theoretical suggestion is that economies may have comparative institutional advantages as far as innovation patterns are concerned" (Soskice, 1997: 76). As set out in

Michael Porter's earlier book *The Competitive Advantage of Nations* (1990), the broad conclusion, supplemented by other sources is that, firstly, the US and the UK are strong in the following:

- Radical innovation in what are considered newly emerging technologies.
- Carrying out sophisticated internationally competitive services.
- Operationalising large complex systems, especially in instances of rapid technological change such as telecommunication systems, defense systems, large software systems, airline systems and large aircraft production.

On the other hand, Germany, Sweden and Switzerland are strong at incremental product and process innovation, often at a scientific leading edge in established technologies, especially machinery and chemicals. Nevertheless, these are still relatively complex products, involving complex production processes and after-sales service and frequently close long-term customer links.

More recently, Jiang and Zhang (2018)[1] have noted the same point, that "the U.S., Germany and South Korea are three well-known innovative countries with high rankings in global innovation index ranking but different politico-economic institutional contexts." They observe that in the knowledge subsystem, all three of these countries are successful in their own domains: in the year 2016, the Republic of Korea (ROK), Germany and the United States governments increased their R&D as proportions of GDP by 4.2% (ROK), 2.9% (Germany) and 2.7% (the US). In turn their private companies funded scientific research by shares of 75.4%, 65.6% and 62.3%, respectively. These countries are in the top three globally, with the US generating some 2,077 scientific and technology citations, followed by

---

[1]These authors also make the methodological case for the comparative method: "single case studies help to reveal the process and reasons for building an innovative country in detail, but focusing on a single country may fail to discover the country's comparative advantages and disadvantages for innovation development. For example, the strong government intervention of South Korea in innovation development has been acknowledged in some literature, but without being compared to countries with less intervention, the adaptability of the South Korea model is hard to clarify" (p. 2), adding that "Comparative studies help to summarize the common factors for innovation, and institution is seen as an important one" (Ibid.).

the ROK and Germany at 1,131 and 576 citations each (Jiang and Zhang, 2018: 7). While the US operates under an "Anglo-Saxon" liberal market-style economy, Germany operates within the European continental social market economy system, while South Korea is a state-developing market economy system. The extent of American liberalism should not be taken for complete laissez-faire, however. As early as the 19th century, through the Morrill Land-Grants Acts (1862) which led to the subsidization of leading research universities, most notably Cornell University and the MIT. World War II and the Cold War (as seen in Chapter 2), saw even more government involvement and funding in US scientific endeavour with buy-in by both the White House and Congress. The 1980s also saw the Bayh-Dole Act which established procedures for assigning ownership of IP to research institutions in instances where specific discoveries had been made by that institution while contracted by a federal agency. Moreover, the 1990s have seen government support for scientific research grow, with flagship programs such as the Human Genome Project (Jiang and Zhang, 2018: 3–4). As Porter (1990: 377) had observed, in the 1990s, the US government was unmatched in its capacity to create incentives for new inventions and industries. Germany, on the other hand, was the foremost country in improving and upgrading pre-existing technologies in already established industries. This has its own drawbacks. For example Soskice noted a pattern of German banks moving their concentration to London and away from Frankfurt due to the comparative advantage offered by England's relatively looser framework without the presence of veto-possessing work councils who also have managerial influence.

> "All [German banks] believe that domestic business, which is seen as requiring the same competences as high quality manufacturing — namely long-term relationships and high skills throughout the workforce — is best kept in Germany. But international operations, needing the ability to hire and fire mobile and gifted professionals and reward them appropriately, can be organized more easily in London" (Soskice, 1997: 77).

The same is true for technology companies as in the same time period, three of Germany's largest biochemistry companies (BASF, Bayer and Hoechsht) closed operations in Germany and put their focus on the US. Noticeably, though, they retained some research components for high-value added chemicals in the home country (Soskice, 1997: 77). This effectively demonstrates the outlook of companies as one of tapping competitive advantages of various states for different processes in the value chain.

On one hand, following the Nobel Prize-winning work of institutional economist Douglas North,[2] many scholars are interested in the role of institutions qua rules of the game (North, 1990). Formal institutions are rules which are expressly written and codified and accepted precisely on that basis. These have been implemented to enact economic and legal frameworks. This insistence on property rights protections — and most importantly its enforcement — has secured the "the success of capitalism in the West" (Liu *et al.*, 2012: 213).[3] Informal institutions, on the other hand, are those socially-embedded rules which are not codified into legal regulations. Both sorts of institutions influence the institutional environments and the organisations embedded in them (Liu *et al.*, 2012: 212). Particularly regarding innovation, Jiang and Zhang have recently extended Leoncini's innovation system model, which broke down the innovation system into four subsystems: knowledge, technical products, markets and institutions. The knowledge subsystem takes into consideration scientific and technical knowledge that is generated by research entities. The technical product subsystem takes into account knowledge as input to produce technical products of enterprises. In the market subsystem, innovative products are eventually brought to commercialisation. Through certain rules, the institution subsystem will either promote or inhibit the innovation process. As Jiang and Zhang see it, however, the theory had the advantage of clearly anatomising the innovation system but still seeing the institutions as merely one subsystem among others while neglecting its relationship to policies. Jiang and Zhang's (2018: 4) work seek to further expand the theory by conceptualising institutions as the central structure to innovation systems by which the content and execution of policies for each subsystem (knowledge, product and market) are bounded.

As a country and an economic phenomenon experiencing both institutional transformation and technological leadership, post-1978 China offers an interesting case study. This is especially so when we look at sub-national levels. Recent research notes variations in propensities of technological entrepreneurship in China and makes the argument that regional-level entrepreneurship policies have had significant influence on entrepreneurial outcomes (Liu *et al.*, 2012: 212). This is made more salient by the decisive point in time from which the country took up its Reform and Opening Up

---

[2]1993, shared with Robert Fogel.
[3]This should be relevant to Chapter 1, among the variables discussed by Diamond, but which he deems as being necessary but insufficient for technology to take root and be sustained.

Policy: the move from Maoism to the post-1978 policy paradigm shored up entrepreneurial activity as personal enterprise was no longer taboo due to political ideology (Liu *et al.*, 2012: 211). There is evidence that enterprise took off even before it was granted permission by official policy overhaul with the communes becoming unbundled autonomously by farmers before the commune system was disbanded by law (Ndzendze, 2020: 4). This reflects the salience of informal institutions which, it seems, lead formal ones. As a result, the PRC has garnered a reputation as one of the most entrepreneur-friendly countries globally (Liu *et al.*, 2012: 211). Moreover, international guanxi leads to government intervention, which leads to the attainment of local guanxi. Overall, then, the presence of guanxi has a positive correlation with high-tech start-ups ("guanxi" is a cultural construct that involves a unique interpersonal relationship which is deeply rooted in Chinese culture that signifies deep trust between individuals). In their study, Liu *et al.* (2012) view guanxi as an example of a China-specific informal institution since such relationships are part of the Chinese social fabric. In their study, the phenomenon enhances interpersonal trust, which in turn undergirds high performance by firms. Previous studies had also drawn similar findings (Sachs, 2005; Xiao and Tsui, 2007; Wong and Tjosvold, 2010). For example, an examination of Chinese high-tech firms by Xiao and Tsui finds that social capital (another conception of guanxi) is a key variable among brokers' performance (Xiao and Tsui, 2007), and a later study of 100 paired competitors operating in various industries in Shanghai shows that guanxi diminishes conflict, and as such enhances effectiveness in partnerships (Wong and Tjosvold, 2010). What sets Liu and colleagues apart is the fact that theirs was among the first to explicitly study the role of guanxi on innovation. They hypothesised and proved that "formal and informal institutions influence each other reciprocally, and that they jointly influence high technology innovation." This allows them to prove a synthetic model that integrates the symbiotic influence of formal and informal institutions (p. 216).

As a realisation of informal institutions, they conceptualise guanxi as a multidimensional construct that consists of local guanxi and international guanxi; in this regard,

> "local guanxi takes the form of intensive business contacts with local players, including end users, suppliers, regulators, and local governmental officials. International guanxi manifests itself in the international connections of high technology entrepreneurs

acquired during international exposure, such as education or work experience in foreign countries as well as cooperation with partners abroad" (pp. 216–217).

In terms of their findings, Liu *et al.* (2012) note that international guanxi plays an important role in innovation in China's high-tech startups potentially due to the status and regard given to innovation within modern-day China compared to both developing as well as developed economies. China's tech startups are likely to make use of overseas connections either through joint development of products or through localising existing product sets (Liu *et al.*, 2012: 222).

Furthermore, overseas returnees' intermediary roles which include either importing products or transferring technologies "give a competitive advantage over local Chinese firms which do not possess international guanxi" (p. 222). These activities are observed as inviting "imitative innovation" (Liu *et al.*, 2012: 222) for which China gained a reputation. As seen, one of the definitive features of innovation is the risk it entails. Thus, through international guanxi, time required to innovate is arguably shortened and risks associated with innovation are diminished (Woywode and Xing, 2012: 222). According to one of their respondents,

> "We highly welcome Chinese nationals who live abroad to return and embark upon a new successful career in our park. We also encourage them to maintain their contacts abroad. They do not need to invest 100% of their time here [China]. Links overseas are important" (in Liu *et al.*, 2012: 222).

Indeed, in this regard, China is not alone, as the imitative strategies were similarly utilised by the former Soviet states in Central and Eastern Europe (see Minniti and Lévesque, 2010). On the other hand, the reverse (i.e., local guanxi) also holds. For example, a 2006 study of 75 United Kingdom and American manufacturers in China discovered a strong and continuing role for guanxi networks in the pursuit of suitable local customers (Millington *et al.*, 2006). On the other hand, there can be such a phenomenon as too much internationalisation, with overseas technology entrepreneurs who have been absent from China for an extended period likely to struggle with acquiring valuable local guanxi. In turn, this induces limited market knowledge as the lack of local guanxi may inhibit their innovation. The technology entrepreneurs from their sample, on the other hand, shared the difficulty experienced in doing business with local firms. To remedy this, local governments can intervene in the guanxi acquisition process of high technology entrepreneurs (Liu *et al.*, 2012: 223). Thus, governments can play the important role of assisting high-tech entrepreneurs to reach consumers and thereby curtail the costs associated with searching for and acquiring customers (Liu *et al.*, 2012: 223). This is not without its critiques, however. Empirical evidence suggests that even though R&D subsidisation encourages further R&D investment by private enterprises with political connections, this investment is observed in even high levels in firms without such connections (Jiang and Zhang, 2018: 3). This still demonstrates the effectiveness of R&D — different levels of it are seen when government is involved. By contrast, lack of government involvement in R&D represents a lack of public leadership in research which in turn is a major hindrance to private involvement. Empirical investigations into developing countries note that they lack both sorts of R&D and may in fact need an initial demonstration of government commitments:

> "Industrial R&D is most often lagging behind, in spite of several government incentives. Business expenditures on R&D (BERD), as a consequence, are small in absolute terms and as a percentage of GDP. The paper suggests that several factors explain this situation, including badly designed incentives, reduced government commitment to these incentives, lack of appropriate vertical STI policies, and high levels of causal ambiguity around specific policy incentives. This paper argues that increased government commitment, policy evaluation and the implementation of vertical STI policies aimed at creating new sectors can solve the technological stalemate" (Niosi, 2010: 250).

Thus, well-planned and actively executed Science, Technology and Innovation (STI) policies facilitate the attainment of high economic and social development among the developed and lead to higher levels of catch-up by the developing (Nour, 2013: 153). With regard to a notable laggard in terms of technological development, Nour's (Nour, 2013: 157) investigation finds that the financial resources designated towards growing STI (measured through R&D as a share of GDP), implying that (like many African countries) Sudan's government earmarks only a small amount of funds towards STI, especially when compared to the OECD, the EU, East Asia and Pacific and even the global average (World). Notably, the years between 2005 and 2009 saw the rate of R&D as a proportion of GDP in Sudan at only 0.28% — far below the best-performing (OECD), average (World) and

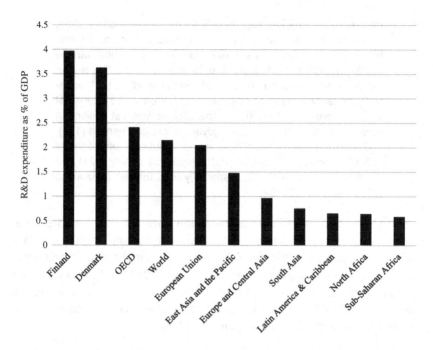

Fig. 4.1.  Select countries and regions by R&D expenditure (2005–2009).
*Source*: Chart by authors. Data obtained from Nour (2013).

even lower-than-average performers (sub-Saharan Africa) at 2.4, 2.14 and 0.58% respectively (see Fig. 4.1).

The country's minimal devotion of resources to scientific research is contrasted by the cases of Sweden and Finland, the two foremost countries in R&D expenditure at 3.62 and 3.96% (see Fig. 4.1). Following its regime change in 2019, it is possible that the country's scientific outlook may receive a positive change. Indeed, among the most notable facets of its October 2020-signed normalisation of relations agreements with the US and Israel are scientific cooperation agreements. Sudanese officials welcomed the move, due to the promise that Israel will provide agricultural technology that will enhance the country's harvests (Atit and Biajo, 2020). Overall Sudan appears to perform poorly due to a number of reasons, at the core of which is a lack of governmental direction and institutional framework to guide innovation policy goals:

> "Mainly, it has a weak position in terms of innovation index and five input enabler pillars including: institutions, human capital,

infrastructure, market sophistication, business sophistication, output pillars: scientific output and creative output and innovation efficiency index. Of the general ranking of the whole sample of 125 economies included in the calculation of the GII, Sudan exhibits a weak position in terms of institution pillar (121), especially, because of its weak position in the bottom place in terms of political environment (125), and the second weakest position in terms of political stability (124), government effectiveness (124), and also a weak position in terms of regulatory environment (120), especially rule of law (123), regulatory quality (121) and business environment (82), especially time to start a business (102)" (Nour, 2013: 162).

Sub-state actors and informal institutions are similarly noted as their findings indicate that R&D had an important role in satisfying the needs of economic development, the development of local technologies and adaptation to imported foreign technologies (Nour, 2013: 167). However, and perhaps predictably, the contribution of R&D seems to be constrained mainly by a lack of finance, being placed ahead even of human resources (researchers and qualified workers in R&D fields).

"We find that the main problem hindering R&D includes the lack of finance from the public sector; lack of management and organization ability; lack of coordination and weak relationships, networks, consistency and cooperation between universities and higher education institutions on the one side and the productive sector (agriculture, industry, services) on the other side; lack of R&D culture; lack of finance from the private sector; lack of favorable conditions and the necessary facilities; lack of awareness and appreciation of the economic values of R&D; lack of human resources (researchers and qualified workers in R&D fields)" (Nour, 2013: 167).

Having reviewed how governance affects technological development, in the following section, we review the other direction of this relationship by looking at the role of technology as a mediating variable and as a tool in political action.

## 4.3   AI, Big Data and Elections

Modern political campaigns rely on the toolbox and data offered by technology corporations such as Facebook and Google, leaders in the online advertising industry bolstered by 4IR technologies such as AI and Big Data which allow them to carry out microtargeting wherein the various campaigns can modify and customise their message to specific models based on political leanings. This is derived from articles the voter has read in the past, videos they have watched, and search histories. Thus rather than uniformly putting out city-wide TV advertisements, microtargeted political commercials are cost-effective precisely because they can seek out of voters to the level of the individual (Wakabayashi and Goldmacher, 2019). In the wake of this, in October 2019, Twitter made the announcement that it would ban all political advertising from its platform. In turn, Twitter's decision was widely interpreted as a response to the controversy caused by Facebook when it refused to de-platform a reportedly false video issued by the Trump campaign accusing a family member of a Democratic presidential candidate of improper business conduct in Ukraine (Wakabayashi and Goldmacher, 2019). Twitter's decision also led to Google's decision to do the same in November 2019.

> "Political advertisers will be able to aim their messages at people based on their age, gender or location. Google will also allow ads to be targeted to people based on the content of websites they visit. However, the ads can no longer be directed to specific audiences based on their public voter records or political affiliations categorized as "left-leaning," "right-leaning," or "independent"" (Wakabayashi and Goldmacher, 2019).

In an email circular to the various campaigns, Google clarified the new rules, including that "election ads will no longer be allowed to target what is called 'affinity audiences' that look like other groups that campaigns might want to target," and that "campaigns can also no longer upload their own lists of people to show ads" (Wakabayashi and Goldmacher, 2019). Reaching new audiences would be more challenging to reach, as Google also banned remarketing, or serving targeted adverts to devices which had previously advertised a campaign's website. This could also reverse what has been one of the unintended outcomes of microtargeting: political balkanisation which have led to partisan tribalism.

There have been numerous studies looking at the growth, impact and significance of digital advertising in the political process. For example, Williams and Gulati studied the 2012 and 2016 campaigns in terms of traditional and digital advertising. In this regard, they found that both campaigns' expenditures on digital media had grown over time. The greatest growth in digital advertising expenditures between 2012 and 2016 had grown most on the Republican side (Williams and Gulati, 2017: 1). Another study by Fowler *et al.* (2018) drew on data from Facebook and television from the Wesleyan Media Project and found that the majority of candidates advertise on Facebook than on television. Going a step further, they sought to identify the within-case variation of uses of either television or Facebook in the 2018 congressional, gubernatorial and state legislative elections. In this regard, they found that of those candidates who used both mediums, Facebook adverts are more prevalent in the early stages of the campaign and tends to be less focused on emphasising the negative aspects of the opposition (negative campaigning), but also tends to be less issue-focused and more partisan than TV advertising (Fowler *et al.*, 2018: 1).

Spenkuch and Toniatti (2018), on the other hand, sought to study the persuasiveness of political adverts in presidential elections between 2004 and 2012. Their findings demonstrated that total political advertising has a minimal to no effect on total voter turnout (Spenkuch and Toniatti, 2018: 1981). Nevertheless, they found that there was a positive correlation with advertising expenditure and candidates' vote shares. Their estimates, therefore, indicate that a regression discontinuity design shows that commercials influence electoral outcomes by changing the partisan composition of the voters (Spenkuch and Toniatti, 2018: 1981).

Many of these studies thus look at the US elections from within the US domestic context. Among internationally-minded studies, the interest is on the role of international dynamics on the actions of incumbents during the electoral cycle. But internationally, Big Data analytics demonstrates an interesting effect. In Figs. 4.2. to 4.5. we produce charts with data drawn from Google Trends. The undeniable trend from all four charts is that the candidate who gets the most searches goes on to win the election, despite both candidates getting an uptick in November, the month of the election (with the eventual winner experiencing the most amount of searches). Indeed past results show that the eventual winner starts getting the most amount of searches as early as January of the election year.

The migratory pattern of politics towards the digital sphere has been recognised for some decades, with the digital sphere adding a new but important dimension. This was captured most dramatically in a decision by *Time* magazine to name as the 2006 Person of the Year, not any political figure as had been custom. Instead, for that year the title went to "You". The editors of the magazine did this in recognition of the increasing levels of empowerment that individuals gained due to growth in internet access.

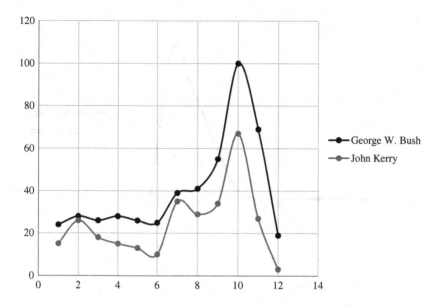

Fig. 4.2. Worldwide Google searches for US Presidential Candidates, 2004. Sourced from Google Trends. Chart by authors.

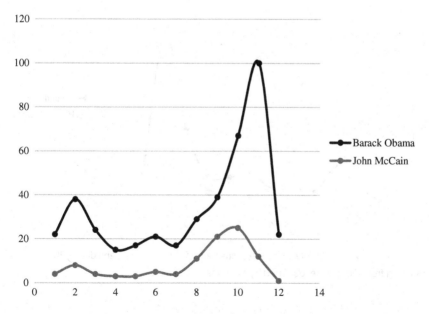

Fig. 4.3. Worldwide Google searches for US Presidential Candidates, 2008. Sourced from Google Trends. Chart by authors.

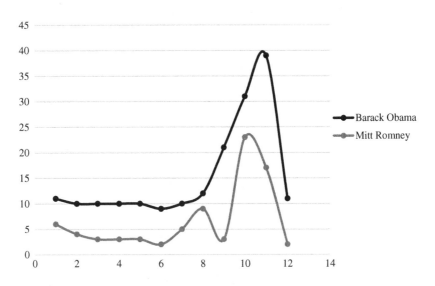

Fig. 4.4.	Worldwide Google searches for US Presidential Candidates, 2012.
Sourced from Google Trends. Chart by authors.

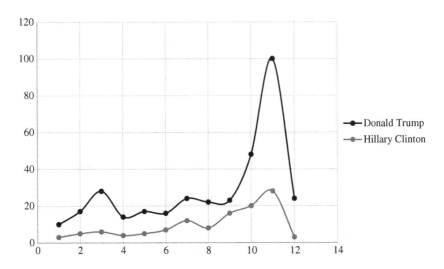

Fig. 4.5.	Worldwide Google searches for US Presidential Candidates, 2016.
Sourced from Google Trends. Chart by authors.

In political science and economics, it is generally recognised that collective action is a very difficult phenomenon to execute due to the costs generally involved. Indeed, "the costs of collective action help explain why mass movements historically have been so rare, even when large sections of a population might share the same views and goals" (Rice and Zegart, 2018: 66). This is changing, however. As Condoleezza Rice and Amy Zegart put it in their book *Political Risk: Facing the Threat of Global Insecurity in the Twenty-First Century*:

> "Connective technologies ... have sent the costs of collective action plummeting, making it easier, safer, faster, and cheaper for like-minded people to find one another, share information, organize, and take individual actions in loosely coordinated ways toward a common goal, even across geopolitical differences" (2018: 66).

This was demonstrated by the "Arab Spring" in 2011. Beginning with a Tunisian vendor setting himself on fire in protest of the Tunisian regime's abuses in 2010, it quickly became a democracy-seeking movement in the historically non-democratic countries of the Middle East; large protests seeking regime change, many of which were organised through social media outlets such as Facebook and Twitter, soon broke out in Libya (where Muammar Gaddafi was removed), Yemen (where Ali Abdullah was removed); Morocco, Jordan, Kuwait, Lebanon and Oman (all five countries saw major reforms), and minor ones in Bahrain, Saudi Arabia and Mauritania which were not quite as successful (Ndzendze, 2017: 24–25). Though the Arab Spring uprisings saw different results, ranging from democratisation (e.g., Tunisia and Egypt), civil war (e.g., Libya, Syria and Yemen) and little to no effect (e.g., Saudi Arabia and Sudan), it nonetheless showed the power in the hands of the citizenry in the wake of new technologies, particularly social media. As Rice and Zegart put it,

> "When you think of twenty-first century political risk, imagine instead a crowded landscape of different actors, not just dictators banning soft drinks and commandeering oil rigs. This landscape includes individuals wielding cell phones, local officials issuing city ordinances, terrorists detonating truck bombs ... and many more" (Rice and Zegart, 2018: 15).

In today's world, activists have new, more and more powerful technological tools that can dramatically increase the speed and scale of their efforts and the odds that they will succeed (Rice and Zegart, 2018: 16). Indeed, individuals need not be members of organised groups or even see themselves as activists to pose risks — they need only be "bystanders with 280 characters and a cellular network" (Rice and Zegart, 2018: 17). On the other hand, state actors remain the most potent and sophisticated cybersecurity threats, most notably the US, Russia, China, Iran and the DPRK (Rice and Zegart, 2018: 51). This sets the scene for rivalries to play themselves out on the cybersphere, with official government systems being major targets. The US government alone repels millions of attempted cyber attacks on its networks each month from the militaries of other governments and their militaries (Rice and Zegart, 2018: 49). The year 2016 was a particularly watershed moment for one of the most studied democracies in the world. Earlier in the year, the mysterious group Shadow Brokers began releasing a mass of "secret computer vulnerabilities that had been stolen from the NSA" (Rice and Zegart, 2018: 50). However, that same year the Russian government conduced never before seen "influence operations to disrupt the American presidential system and undermine American democracy" (Rice and Zegart, 2018: 50). Moreover:

> "Russia's efforts included hacking the campaign-related websites and servers, releasing data from those breaches online, penetrating multiple state and local electoral boards, disseminating propaganda overtly through Russian state-backed media outlets RT and Sputnik, and inflaming social cleavages by covertly spreading deceptive information with botnets, fake accounts, and unwitting users on American and social media platforms" (Rice and Zegart, 2018: 50).

In previous, less fractured times, there might have been a strong, united response from the US. But these were no ordinary times, with many Republican leaders and voters showing reluctance to take on Russia as this would mean defying and delegitimising a Republican president, according to Microsoft President Brad Smith and co-author Carol Ann Browne in their 2019 book *Tools and Weapons: The Promise and the Peril of the Digital Age*. The dichotomous metaphor used by the authors in the title of the book paints a clear picture of the role of technology in the present era; it cannot be divorced from the actions and designs of those who make use of it. It serves political ends. This has been similarly observed in Kenya, where the practice of democracy (i.e. elections) always carries the prospect of political violence. In "New Information Communication Technologies and

Electoral Violence in Africa", Gwala (2019: 10) observes that new ICTs lead to bi-directional outcomes in elections. For example,

> "Similar to other New ICTs, blogs were utilised to spread hate speech whilst others focused on spreading peace. Noting that since blogs often reflect individual owners' thoughts and views that are susceptible to biasness, it can be difficult for States to impose any form of regulation ... The main problem posed by blogs during the post-election violence is that most of the bloggers had strong opinions that leaned in favour of their preferred candidates or tribal groups" (Gwala, 2019: 53).

And conversely,

> "ICTs were later employed to understand the nature and extent of electoral violence through the identification and mapping of hotspots. In this regard, ICTs came to play an important role in the post-election period following the outbreak of electoral violence due to their capacity to report and disseminate information at a faster rate than traditional media" (Gwala, 2019: 53).

But the analysis also leaves scope for responsible usage; as in the subsequent election (2013), government took a proactive role and made punitive measures against certain actors, including citizens, businesses (network providers) and politicians:

> "At the national and international level, there were many projects that acknowledged the fatal role of hate speech during the elections and sought to counter the speech through calls for peace ... the government also took the helm in countering violence. Through the imposition of a fine or 3-year jail term for those found guilty of hate speech. It mandated mobile operators to register cell phone sim cards for tracing purposes. Politicians were also required to go through a vetting process (sifting for messages of hate speech) through their mobile operators in order to send bulk messages. Furthermore, the government had sent out warnings of prosecution to bloggers and social media users for the use of dangerous language. The Independent Media Council also monitored hate speech radio stations, TV channels, and newspapers. Thus in 2013, the government made significant efforts to counter hate speech through regulations and constant monitoring of the electoral environment" (Gwala, 2019: 60).

Three years later, in a different context, the electoral process was put under scrutiny as the aftermath of the 2016 US election had alerted many stakeholders. For example, a working group at Microsoft contemplated the stakes if a particularly close election might be widely suspected of having been hacked by a foreign government without systematic proof that they had not been. This motivated them to develop such a system and subsequently launch an open source-based software called Microsoft ElectionGuard. In the system, the voter selects the candidates from an electronic screen which is recorded on paper ballots printed. The voter can retain this paper as proof of having voted. More importantly, this proof contains a unique, algorithmically-derived encryption which can be traced online to verify one's vote and ensure that it is accurately recorded and remains unchanged and thus free from fraud (Smith and Browne, 2019: 87).

The placement of actors' intentions (be they foreign governments or domestic in their origin) at the core of political outcomes to be produced by the new technologies has also been the subject of increasing contemplation by election regulators when it comes to blockchain technology's most noted application in recent years: cryptocurrency. There are presently more than a thousand cryptocurrencies in the world today, though the most popular remains bitcoin. What sets them apart is the anonymity and transparency they offer — though this occurs on a spectrum, which is where the dilemma presents itself: "since they are currently (relatively) unregulated, it is unclear in many countries whether political finance transactions using cryptocurrencies are allowed" (Institute for Democratic and Electoral Assistance (IDEA), 2019: 7). Essentially, the dilemma is whether cryptocurrency should be considered as currency or, alternatively, whether it constitutes a class of its own with no precedent and therefore without possibility of classification. The distinction is crucial since rules and regulations are different for cash as opposed to other "in-kind" donations (IDEA, 2019: 11). Russian activities in the 2016 US election were partly funded through cryptocurrencies. This is important as the US, along with 68% of countries in the world, bans foreign donations to political organisations and 56% prohibit foreign donations to candidates.

This is where the spectrum becomes salient as cryptocurrencies which trade-off transparency for anonymity support oversight agencies, and in this regard legislatures are likely in favour of the use of public ledgers to track the provenance of the funds in question (IDEA, 2019: 16). Such policies have already found interest in countries such as Mexico and Kenya. In the former, there has been advocacy for funneling *all* political monetary transactions through cryptocurrencies, "or otherwise promoting identities through a public ledger," while in Kenya cryptocurrencies have been used in elections to ensure voter integrity (IDEA, 2019: 16). But these are still the early stages. The experience of Iceland is instructive. In 2012, the country's civilian population crowdsourced the creation of a referendum on a new constitution which had also been drafted from the ground-up which proposed environmental protections, international human rights law, refugees and wealth distribution. The document gained the approval of two-thirds of voters. "The participatory nature of its writing sets it apart from other similar documents," observe Kinna *et al.* (2016: 1). However, the document ultimately failed as it was rejected by the government of the day.

The substance of the chapter is nonetheless instructive. In coming decades, the political arena is going to experience major changes at the behest of AI and other emerging technologies — it is to be characterised by two extremes at different points: participation and accountability on one end, and confinement of the political space by governments on the other. Ultimately, however, the core questions of politics will remain as they have for thousands of years. Questions of power, representativeness, distribution, transparency and caution against foreign influence are going to tower over the political process. Yet is it also clear that leadership is being provided by what are traditionally marginal countries who have been petri dishes and laboratories for policy measures meant to curtail nefarious actors and to promote the social good. These experiments are in themselves not perfect, but they show the urgent need for legal frameworks that keep pace with these changes. They need elevation and broadening through international law. One of the potential consequences of this is an unpredictable global environment that may breed conditions for conflict. This is dealt with in Chapter 6, whereas some of the encouraging steps being taken by regions are reviewed in Chapter 7.

# References

Atit, Michael and Biajo, Nabeel. 2020 (October 26). "Sudan: Normalization With Israel Was US Condition But Will Be Beneficial," *VOA News*. URL: https://www.voanews.com/africa/south-sudan-focus/sudan-normalization-israel-was-us-condition-will-be-beneficial (Accessed: 21 November 2020).

Fowler, Erika Franklin, Ridout, Travis N., and Franz, Michael M. 2018. "Political Advertising in 2016: The Presidential Election as Outlier?," *The Forum*, 14(4): 445–469.

Gwala, Noxolo. 2019. "New Information Communication Technologies and Electoral Violence in Africa." MA Thesis: Wits University.

Institute for Democracy and Electoral Assistance. 2019. "Cryptocurrencies and Political Finance," *International IDEA Discussion Paper 2/2019*. URL: https://www.idea.int/sites/default/files/publications/cryptocurrrencies-and-political-finance.pdf (Accessed: 28 December 2019).

Jiang, Xuan and Zhang, Peipei. 2018. "Institutions, policies and diverse innovation systems: Experiences from the US, Germany and South Korea," *Journal of Asian Public Policy*, DOI: 10.1080/17516234.2018.1541116.

Kinna, Ruth, Prichard, Alex and Swann, Thomas. 2016 (October 28). "Iceland's crowd-sourced constitution: Hope for disillusioned voters everywhere," *The Conversation*.

Liu, Yipeng, Woywode, Michael, and Xing, Yijun. 2012. "High technology start-up innovation and the role of *guanxi*: An explorative study in China from an institutional perspective," *Prometheus*, 30(2), 211–229.

Millington, Andrew, Eberhardt, Markus, and Wilkinson, Barry. 2006. "Guanxi and supplier search mechanisms in China," *Human Relations*, 59(4): 505-–531.

Minniti, Maria and Lévesque, Moren 2010. "Entrepreneurial types and economic growth," *Journal of Business Venturing*, 25(3), 305–314.

Ndzendze, Bhaso. 2017. *Beginner's Dictionary of Contemporary International Relations*. Pretoria: NLSA.

Ndzendze, Bhaso. 2020. "'Catching Up After Half a Millennium': Jeffrey Sachs on the Chinese Development Model," *Centre for Africa-China Studies Occasional Paper No. 9*. URL: http://www.cacs.org.za/wp-content/uploads/2020/05/CACS-Occasional-Paper-no-9-desktop.pdf (Accessed: 22 November 2020).

Niosi, Jorge. 2010. "Rethinking science, technology and innovation (STI) institutions in developing countries," *Innovation*, 12(3), 250–268.

Nour, Samia Satti Osman Mohamed. 2013. "Science, Technology and Innovation Policies in Sudan," *African Journal of Science, Technology, Innovation and Development*, 5(2), 153–169.

Porter, M.E. 1990. *The Competitive Advantage of Nations*. London: MacMillan.

Rice, Condoleezza and Zegart, Amy. 2018. *Political Risk: Facing the Threat of Global Insecurity in the Twenty-First Century*. London: Weidenfeld and Nicolson.

Sachs, Jeffrey. 2005. *The End of Poverty*. New York: Penguin.

Smith, Brad and Browne, Carol Ann. 2019. *Tools and Weapons: The Promise and the Peril of the Digital Age*. London: Hodder and Stoughton.

Soskice, David. 1997. "German technology policy, innovation, and national institutional frameworks," *Industry and Innovation*, 4(1), 75–96.

Spenkuch, Jörg L. and Toniatti, David. 2018. "Political Advertising and Election Results," *Quarterly Journal of Economics*, 133(4), 1981–2036.

Wakabayashi, Daisuke and Goldmacher, Shane. 2019. "Google Policy Change Upends Online Plans for 2020 Campaigns," *New York Times*. URL: https://www.nytimes.com/2019/11/20/technology/google-political-ads-targeting.html (Accessed: 22 November 2020).

Williams, Christine B. and Gulati, Girish J. "Jeff". 2017. "Digital Advertising Expenditures in the 2016 Presidential Election," *Social Science Computer Review.* 36(4): 406–421.

Wong, Alfred and Tjosvold, Dean 2010. "Guanxi and conflict management for effective partnering with competitors in China," *British Journal of Management*, 21(3), 772–788.

Xiao, Zhixing and Tsui, Anne 2007. "When brokers may not work: The cultural contingency of social capital in Chinese high technology firms," *Administrative Science Quarterly*, 52(1), 1–31.

## Datasets

US presidential candidate searches, 2004 (worldwide). 2020. URL: https://trends.google.com/trends/explore?date= all&q=%2Fm%2F0cqt90,%2Fm%2F02mjmr,%2Fm%2F09b6zr (Accessed: 18 January 2020).

US presidential candidate searches, 2009 (worldwide). 2020. URL: https://trends.google.com/trends/explore?date=all&q=%2Fm%2F02mjmr,%2Fm%2F0bymv (Accessed: 18 January 2020).

US presidential candidate searches, 2012 (worldwide). 2020. URL: https://trends.google.com/trends/explore?date=all&q=%2Fm%2F02mjmr,%2Fm%2F0271_s (Accessed: 18 January 2020).

US presidential candidate searches, 2016 (worldwide). 2020. URL: https://trends.google.com/trends/explore?date=all&q=%2Fm%2F0cqt90,%2Fm%2F0d06m5 (Accessed: 18 January 2020).

# Infrastructure, Industrialisation and Development

# 5

**Abstract**

Infrastructure provides an interface between international relations and technology (both traditional and emerging) as it shapes patterns in regionalisation, national security thinking, foreign assistance and economic development, among others. As such, this chapter examines data on hard infrastructure as an international economic and technological phenomenon through comparative assessments of infrastructural competitiveness. It places emphasis on the relationship between ICT infrastructure and economic growth, showing mixed results when it comes to the causal relationship between Development of Telecommunications Infrastructure (DTI) inputs and economic growth outcomes. Through showcasing the emerging literature which problematises some of the assumptions on the infrastructure-economic growth nexus, the chapter thereby notes the differing patterns of access to infrastructure within countries which reflect intra-country inequities that in turn determine dissemination of 4IR technologies. This is particularly important as the chapter observes the increasing rate at which 4IR technologies have been tapped by governments for their post-COVID recoveries.

**Keywords**: 5G; critical acquisition framework; DTI; infrastructure; ICT; IoT; smart infrastructure

## 5.1 Introduction

Infrastructure is integral to international relations processes. Most directly, it is the physical interface of regional integration for the movement of people and goods to facilitate trade and tourism. When we consider the rate of globalisation which has taken shape in the past century, the pattern of growth is accompanied by accumulations and innovations in rail and airplanes, which have made the world smaller. The introduction of the Internet has required more "hard" infrastructure, not less, through undersea cables which are the backbone of the global communications highway. Similarly, 5G stands to see more hardware being installed as discussed in Chapter 1. Countries are incentivised to invest in infrastructure not only to ensure internal efficiency in commerce and access to government services but to also catalyse exports, attract tourists and foreign investment. This final facet of IR — infrastructure — is notable in the comparative manner it manifests through global ranking. Inherently political, China's announcement of its Belt and Road Initiative in 2013 garnered reaction and concern not only in the US, but also in India and Japan. The latter two countries took the opportunity presented by the occasion of the African Development Bank annual general meetings in India in 2017 to announce their own international mega infrastructure project known as the Asia-Africa Growth Corridor (AAGC). In turn, Africa's own infrastructural plans have been wedded to its ambitions of reversing what has been a hitherto marginal role in international trade despite its vast mineral wealth. Crucially, these plans seek to attain greater intracontinental trade, with just a 1% gain in such trade expected to lead to growth by US$70 billion, the equivalent of all foreign aid flowing into the continent (African Union, 2013).

On the reverse end of the competitive poise on infrastructure is cooperation, with the international community identifying the need to help those who require global assistance since the turn of the millennium. Through its Millennium Development Goals and subsequently, through the SDGs (particularly SDG 9), the United Nations has sought to encourage investment in the sustainable catching up of LDCs in infrastructure and industrialisation.

Meta-analytically, infrastructure global value chain inputs are a matter of interest for sceptics who operate from an international political economy perspective; with the industry representing 6% of global GDP and workforce in 2019 (Castagnino *et al.*, 2020; 2019: 2). On the other hand, scholars and practitioners of international law take an interest in issues around the harmonisation of standards, especially in an age of rapid climate change. Yet more change is on the horizon, with the nature of infrastructure itself undergoing transformation, with new patterns in the enactment of smart city strategies by both developed and developing worlds. In such a context, it is necessary to take a step back and consider the essential elements of infrastructure.

To be sure, infrastructure can be an ambiguous term. But the most widely used conceptualisation of infrastructure entails the basic physical structures and facilities that are needed for the function of societies and businesses. Infrastructure is thus to be understood by the forms it comes in. The first sort is the distinction between hard and soft infrastructure; in the first instance we can count roads, bridges, railways, harbours, canals, docks and communications, whereas in the latter we can count the various institutions that maintain the economic, health and social standards of a country. In the conventional scientific literature, infrastructure is thus distilled to its physical components or assets. The list thus incorporates such items as energy plants and distribution, transport, telecommunications, water and sanitation as well as the safe disposal of waste. Various scholars (e.g., Prud'homme [2005]; Baldwin and Dixon [2008]) additionally note that infrastructure consists of long-term inputs that are spatially-bound and capital-intensive with ideally long life cycles (Palei, 2015: 169).

Infrastructure, insofar as it is a means towards the carrying out of projects at a national level has largely been seen as a public good, with its provision being largely reliant on the government. Indeed, most major public works are conducted by the government, being paid for by taxes, tolls or user fees. On the other hand, the private sector has played a role in the provision of energy and telecommunications in a number of countries. Nevertheless, these remain subject to public regulation and operate within legal frameworks. At the same time, governments have partnered with private sectors in pursuit of specific projects to co-manage costs. Similarly, governments have partnered with foreign governments towards these ends. Examples here may include the Marshall Plan after WWII, as well as the ultimately ill-fated Ring Road in Afghanistan which received diminishing funding from the US due to the resources being needed in Iraq. In the case of Africa, China has been a repeat partner. The first such partnership was the Tazara Railway, which linked Tanzania and Zambia, but there have been numerous since, including SGR in Kenya, Ethiopia and Djibouti, as well as a major bridge in Mozambique and some refurbishing work in Angola. International organisations and international financial institutions have come to the fore. Observed the World Bank CFO in 2015:

> "Infrastructure is now front and center with the OECD, G20, G77, and the IMF. The multilateral development banks are ratcheting up their work on infrastructure. Some are increasing their balance sheets (ADB), some are growing their lending (WBG), many are setting up project preparation facilities (AfDB, EBRD, ADB), and, of course new MDBs like AIIB are specifically focusing on infrastructure" (in Jacobs, 2016: 387)

Infrastructure is also the subject of much social scientific analysis and even criticism, especially in economic terms. The notion of infrastructure-based development is especially prevalent. Here there is an assumed logical nexus between infrastructure and development; with, as we shall see, infrastructure being seen by some scholars as a driver and by others as an indicator of development. The distinction is crucial for the policy implications it carries. This thinking is receiving renewed thinking with the advent of the 4IR technologies, marked by the rise of artificial intelligence, big data and blockchain technology. More emphasis is being placed on the role that these new nodes of technology can play in ushering in more navigable, accessible, environmentally-, and tourist-friendly smart cities. This leap in thinking and priorities is crucial to note. However, as will be seen in the penultimate section of this chapter, this thinking is not universally held due to the qualified nature of access. Among recent events that have taken shape and that will have an impact on global economic discourse and infrastructure rollout is the COVID-19 pandemic which emerged in Wuhan, China, in late 2019 and spread globally in early 2020. Initially slowing down the construction industry due to the global economic lockdowns, early indicators show that we should expect the COVID-19 crisis to expedite the uptake of 4IR infrastructure as governments stimulate their economies, while ensuring post-COVID competitiveness, long-term sustainability through innovation.

Section 5.2 looks at the economics of infrastructure in global comparative perspective. Section 5.3 reviews the Critical Acquisition Framework and the problems it poses on our assumptions about infrastructure as we move into the 4IR. Section 5.4 concludes the chapter with a discussion on new developments around infrastructure in the wake of the 4IR technologies and the COVID-19 pandemic as countries look to a post-pandemic future.

## 5.2 The Economics of Infrastructure in Global Comparative Perspective

Infrastructure investments are said to encourage private-sector investments through a number of mechanisms. One of these is by reducing the costs associated with opening new markets and creating new opportunities for production and trade; while roads reduce costs of transportation, quality ports diminish transaction and by extension, trade costs. They thus give exposure to local firms, and in turn create pressure to innovate from foreign, internationally-leading competitors (Fedderke and Bogetić, 2006:

2). One of the first studies to look into this relationship is Aschauer in his 1989 article "Is Public Expenditure Productive?" published in the *Journal of Monetary Economics* which posited that, almost instantaneously, a decline in public investment across different countries led to a decline in productivity growth (Aschauer, 1989: 177). In similar vein, infrastructural development can be an equalizer for developing countries. The World Bank's *World Development Report* in 1994 highlighted numerous links between infrastructure and development and emphasized that policy measures can not only improve quantity but also the quality of infrastructure in both developed and developing nations. Table 5.1 captures the top 10 countries in the index as of 2019.

According to the WEF's Global Competitiveness report, Hong Kong, Singapore and the Netherlands are home to the best infrastructure in the world. According to the report, the infrastructure in Hong Kong exhibits efficiency and promotes economic development through ensuring that businesses operate efficiently with its estimated 1,138 miles of developed roads, as well as its world-leading air and sea transportation infrastructure. Singapore boasts 1,940 miles of road networks with 99% of these being paved highways (Global Infrastructure Index, 2018). In an effort to decongest the city-state, by the 1990s the government introduced 51 miles of the mass rapid transit system and 6 miles of the light version of the mass rapid transit system. The Netherlands acts as the main point of entry of goods into continental Europe and as a result has emerged as the country with the best

Table 5.1. Countries by global infrastructure index rankings (2019).

| Rank | Country | Infrastructure Index Score |
|---|---|---|
| 1 | Hong Kong | 6.7 |
| 2 | Singapore | 6.5 |
| 3 | Netherlands | 6.4 |
| 4 | Japan | 6.3 |
| 5 | United Arab Emirates | 6.3 |
| 6 | Switzerland | 6.3 |
| 7 | France | 6.1 |
| 8 | Korea | 6.1 |
| 9 | United States | 6.0 |
| 10 | Germany | 6.0 |

*Source*: World Economic Forum 2019.

infrastructure in Europe with high quality of roads, railroad infrastructure, air transport and electricity supply. Other countries with remarkable infrastructure include Japan, United Arab Emirates and Switzerland. Prospectively, "industrial, regional, and national economic systems which do not adopt such technologies in the near future will risk losing their position in the international market" (Pradhan *et al.*, 2014: 402).

A study by Pradhan *et al.* (2014: 401) examined the connection between the development of telecommunications infrastructure (which they term DTI), economic growth as well as four indicators of the operations of developed economies by making use of a panel vector auto-regressive model. The aim of the paper was to find whether there was a causal relationship and to test the long-run correlation between these variables among the G20 countries over the 2001 to 2012 period (2014: 401). Their paper was particularly interested in telephone, internet and broadband usage. In this regard they find evidence pointing to DTI (operationalised through six indicators such as number of telephone land lines per thousand of population; the number of mobile phone subscribers per thousand of population; the number of internet users per thousand of population; number of fixed broadband per thousand of population; a composite index, which is derived through principal component analysis utilizing the first five indicators) causing economic growth. But, importantly, they posit that the causal relationship may possibly be bidirectional whereby DTI leads to direct benefits by lowering transaction costs and improving marketing information, and by creating indirect benefits by accelerating the diffusion of information but at the same time these markets are predictors of the DTI (Pradhan *et al.*, 2014: 401–402). DTI affects economic growth both directly as well as indirectly (see representation in Fig. 5.1).

There are generally four competing schools of thought on infrastructure and economic growth. At the root of these are competing explanations of cause and effect between infrastructure inputs and economic growth and which precedes the other. These schools of thought consist of the supply-leading hypothesis (SLH), the demand-following hypothesis (DFH), the feedback hypothesis (FBH) and the neutrality hypothesis (NLH). The SLH contends that the DTI needs to occur before economic growth. The argument advanced by this school of thought is that DTI is the independent variable from which economic growth follows. Scholars who are proponents of this hypothesis assert that DTI stimulates economic growth through direct support of other infrastructural nodes and factors of production, and in the process substantially improve economic growth. On the other hand,

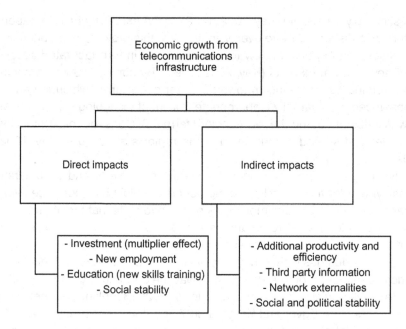

Fig. 5.1.   Impacts of telecommunications infrastructure on economic growth.
*Source*: Adapted from Pradhan *et al.* (2014) with permission from the authors.

proponents of the DFH suggest that causality emanates from economic growth to DTI. In other words, scholars who advance this hypothesis see the DTI as being only a small factor in economic growth and argue that it is essentially a by-product of the economic growth which may already be taking place (Pradhan *et al.*, 2014). Third, there is the FBH which suggests that economic growth and DTI can play a complementary role and in so doing reinforce one another, thus making economic growth and DTI essentially mutually causal. The essence of this view is that telecommunications infrastructure is indispensable to economic growth in modern economies whereas economic growth can lead to more investments in telecommunications infrastructure. The fourth hypothesis argues for the absence of a causal relationship. Notably, the NLH is supported by very few papers.

Nevertheless, the proliferation of these multiple hypotheses represents the diversity of the literature due to the diversity of methodologies and findings on a country-to-country basis. For example, in Brazil the government was reliant upon heavy taxation of exports, particularly agriculture. This in turn was used to fund the industrial infrastructure of well-positioned cities, most notably São Paulo (Kay, 2002: 1092). In the Asian Tigers, rural expenditure was disbursed more evenly. In the end, this proved more conducive for widespread uptake of new technologies and in turn facilitated access and new internal markets (Kay, 2002: 1096). By contrast, South America was dominated by favoritism towards larger scale farms which forged an imbalanced and "partially inappropriate" rollout of technological change as it was diffused among the few (landlord farmers). Consequentially, this led to a delayed spread of innovation in the region's agriculture (Kay, 2002: 1096).

Noting that "Africa must industrialize to end poverty and to generate employment for the 12 million young people who join its labor force every year"[1] the African Development Bank goes on to state that among the continent's developmental retardants is the lack of infrastructure for energy and water supply, and for transportation which would allow companies to flourish in industries where they may have a comparative advantage. In the African continent, South Africa (at #33) was the only country in the top 50 in terms of the Logistics Performance Index in its 2018 ranking. The next best performers were Egypt and Kenya at #67 and #68 respectively. In a 2018 survey by Global Infrastructure Investor Association, the country's airports were scored third after India and Malaysia; South Africa's score of 80 beat even the G8 average score of 65.[2] Ngqura, boasting a year-on-year 129% growth in volumes, also won the 2012 and 2013 Drewry Maritime Research "Fastest Growing Container Terminal in the World" accolade. South Africa's physical infrastructure gained a sizeable boost from the 2010 FIFA World Cup which it hosted (PWC, 2012: 69). However, these have fallen into disuse or disrepair, and in another survey the country's energy efficiency score was only at 32 (p. 25), whilst 78% of respondents in the survey do not believe the country is "doing enough to meet our infrastructure needs" (p. 37). That South Africa is the best performer in the continent puts on display the continent's setbacks. Overall, Africa's infrastructural needs total at between US$130 billion to US$170 billion a year for the next decade,

---

[1] African Development Bank. 2018. "Africa's Infrastructure: Great Potential But Little Impact on Inclusive Growth," African Development Bank. URL: https://www.afdb.org/fileadmin/uploads/afdb/Documents/Publications/2018AEO/African_Economic_Outlook_2018_-_EN_Chapter3.pdf (Accessed: 5 January 2020).

[2] Global Infrastructure Index. 2018. "Public satisfaction and priorities — 2018," URL: https://www.ipsos.com/sites/default/files/ct/news/documents/2018-11/global-infrastructure-index-2018.pdf (Accessed: 5 January 2020).

while its financing gap of US$68 billion to US$108 billion means that it needs external funders. The African Development Bank (AfDB) has noted, however, that African countries today have a wide range of options for tapping funds, in modalities other than foreign aid. These include, for example, creating an "infrastructure asset" class of investment through which governments and international development finance organisations can offer guarantees through "flexible financial engineering," which can diminish the perceived risk of investors. Tax reform will also be needed, according to the AfDB. This is in tune with the African Union's Agenda 2063's position that domestic resource mobilisation (DRM) is crucial to ensuring that the continent's ambitious undertakings are financed in large part through its own largesse. Despite some progress, tax revenue is still below the threshold of 25% of GDP deemed necessary to scale up infrastructure spending on the continent.

## 5.3 Critiquing the Infrastructure–Development Nexus

Differences in infrastructure persist not only between countries but also within countries; different groups have differentiated levels of access to it. In light of this, Gartner (2016: 377) observes critically that "massive investments towards infrastructure projects throughout the developed and developing world convey great confidence in the ability of infrastructure systems to deliver development objectives" and that "such a connection between infrastructure and development is so widely believed that the truncated term of 'infrastructure development' has become common vernacular in academic and policy-making circles." This leads the author to question the very notion that "infrastructure development knowledge has solely been the result of rigorous scientific research, or rather the outcome of a highly politicized process of knowledge creation" (Gartner, 2016: 377):

> "The politics of infrastructure research can be described as a socio-political landscape in which multiple authorities compete to inform infrastructure science and praxis. One's position in this political and perceptual landscape will largely determine one's definition of infrastructure and one's expectation of infrastructure development processes" (Gartner, 2016: 378).

Formed on the basis of a literature review of works on infrastructure development, Gartner's paper (2016: 378) makes the case that despite each perspective offering something significant that forms a piece of the puzzle, the overall scholarship, including the most dominant perspectives among them, "fall short of acknowledging the integral role of power, place, and agency in social, economic, and political change," leading to the author advocating for a more diverse dialogue in the infrastructure development research space. It is against this backdrop that she offers the Critical Acquisition Framework for understanding and incorporating the experiences of marginalised groups in the construction of infrastructure development knowledge, particularly within the context of inequitable societies. The Critical Acquisition Framework draws from literature which has surfaced in the post-development era, namely critical-social theory with its goal of understanding existing power relations in societies, so that there may be transformation to otherwise inequitable systems or ones underlined by "oppressive ideologies".

> "The framework is premised on an actor-based concept of sociopolitical reality, which recognizes societies as being heterogeneous composites of multiple actors; groups of social agents who converge based on shared resource interests ... Between actors therein lie complex patterns of power relations, as some actors are endowed with greater power to pursue their interests and activities over others" (Gartner, 2016: 386).

Particularly, Gartner contends that the processes through which access to infrastructure is obtained need to be better understood to be better understood (Gartner, 2016: 386). In this framework, she proposes the term *acquisition* to refer to:

> "both the act of accessing infrastructure and the act of acquiring objects and services needed to benefit from infrastructure. Some objects need only be acquired once (such as a car), such that people retain permanent ownership and control over infrastructure objects. Other components of infrastructure systems, such as consumable resources like gasoline, need to be continually acquired to power infrastructure systems" (Gartner, 2016: 386).

Gartner's framework asserts the following: assuming that an actor has the will to gain access to an infrastructure system, their power to do so will be determined by their capability. Presuming the actor has the will to access the infrastructure system, their power to access will be mediated "by the match between their existing capabilities and the institutions that regulate access" (pp. 387–388; see Fig. 5.2).

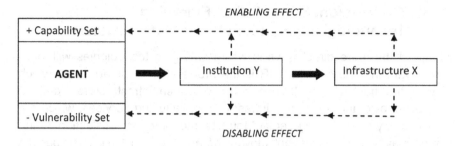

Fig. 5.2.   Gartner's Critical Acquisition Framework.
*Source*: From Gartner (2016), with permission from the author.

Gartner offers the following scenarios:

> "For example, if access to transportation is regulated by market institutions alone, then an actor may only require sufficient financial capabilities in terms of cash to purchase, for example, a ticket for a transportation service. However, if access to transportation is simultaneously regulated by inequitable institutions of gender, one's access to transportation infrastructure can be simultaneously restricted" (p. 388).

It would appear, therefore, that in spite of the empowerment of citizens in possession of digital platforms encountered in the preceding chapter, there are still marginalised individuals and groups precisely because of their distance from infrastructure: "the effects of exercising a large amount of will in the absence of sufficient capability will have limited effect. For this reason, the Critical Acquisition Framework emphasizes the role of capabilities of marginalized groups in the acquisition of infrastructure systems" (Gartner, 2016: 386). Because of its lack of specificity, however, and given the diverse nature of infrastructure, it may be said that one of the weaknesses of this framework is its lack of empiricism (in light of its rather literature-derived origins), its reliance on hypotheticals and reliance only on single case study settings in Peru. This may result in lack of differentiation among different types of infrastructures and societies and forms of marginalisation. Nevertheless, the framework stands to offer some insights when utilised as it will lead to precisely the investigation of these types of questions as we move into the 4IR and 4IR infrastructure; questions which would perhaps otherwise not arise in its absence.

## 5.4  Conclusion: Smart Cities, Emerging Technologies and the Future of Infrastructure

One of the more direct ways in which emerging technologies will interface with infrastructure and IR is the proliferation of smart cities, which will in turn transform the tourism industry. Tourism infrastructure is defined by Jovanović and Ilić as any infrastructure, including services, which are "necessary to meet the needs of tourists and increase satisfaction during their stay at the destination" (Jovanović and Ilić, 2016: 1). Their paper's conclusions suggest that the future of tourism depends on major investments into infrastructural modernisation due to its demonstrated effect in the development of tourism sectors in countries where this sector is lagging (Jovanović and Ilić, 2016: 1). Investing in modernised infrastructure has been found to yield repeat tourism in cross-country studies, including in Greece (Ballis *et al.*, 2017), Indonesia (Vindiana *et al.*, 2020: 126), Nigeria (Adebayo and Iweka, 2014), the UAE (Michael *et al.*, 2019) and the BRICS countries (Bhatt, 2017). A longitudinal study on the BRICS countries particularly demonstrates a return on investment on digital placement in the countries of the tourists (Bhatt, 2017), indicating that countries need to invest in infrastructure competitiveness at home and also keep in tune with the technological development of other countries in order to effectively market themselves in this new era of globalisation.

The COVID-19 pandemic has slowed down economic activity in pursuit of social distancing in order to avoid person-to-person transmission. In the main — although the effects of the pandemic vary widely from one country to another — this has meant construction project delays by an average of 60% while productivity declined by at least 25% with the IMF (2020) anticipating "a recession at least as bad as during the global financial crisis or worse." In the European Union, new health and safety measures have also increased costs per month for every employee from €300 to €350 per worker. Travel across borders have strained and disrupted supply chains (Castagnino *et al.*, 2020: 2). Yet looking ahead, it is clear that many governments across the world are basing substantial portions of their post-COVID recovery plans on infrastructure; this has been the case in countries as diverse as South Africa, Singapore, the US and China:

> "It is likely that additional stimulus packages will be required, beyond those already announced. Underneath the headline figures will come important choices about how to spend that money. Those decisions will impact the speed and depth of recovery,

influence the longer-term health of our economies, and begin to define what our new normal is likely to be once the coronavirus is abated" (Burke, 2020).

Such plans are relying on the multiplier effect, with a University of Maryland study showing that, on average, every dollar invested in infrastructure yields US$3.70 in additional economic growth over a 20-year period. Part of what makes this period unique is the convergence of stimulation-requiring economic recession with the confluence of 4IR technologies. It has been observed for a number of years that 5G needs substantial consideration for cost effectiveness, and an ability to host extremely high volumes of content and traffic demand across IoT devices. Sabella and colleagues posit the need for configurable and flexible networks which they term Flex5Gware (Sabella *et al.*, 2018:199). In a context in which infrastructure inputs, and the economies they were meant to facilitate were already changing, the COVID crisis will mean a faster route to the integration of 4IR technologies and thus a more rapid uptake of 4IR infrastructure. In sum, the future competitiveness of countries (not only in the attraction of new FDI but also in tourism influxes) will depend on countries' uptake of these technologies. Through the crucible of post-COVID-19 economic recoveries by different countries across the globe, substantial rates of unevenness are to be expected.

# References

Adebayo, A.K., and Iweka, A.C. 2014. "Optimizing the Sustainability of Tourism Infrastructure in Nigeria through Design for Deconstruction Framework," Semantic Scholar. URL: https://www.semanticscholar.org/paper/Optimizing-the-Sustainability-of-Tourism-in-Nigeria-Adebayo-Iweka/c5e84240ac01f53d07500cfde664d1d11e8fe14c. Corpus ID: 108134052.

African Development Bank. 2018. "Africa's Infrastructure: Great Potential But Little Impact on Inclusive Growth," African Development Bank. URL: https://www.afdb.org/fileadmin/uploads/afdb/Documents/Publications/2018AEO/African_Economic_Outlook_2018_-_EN_Chapter3.pdf (Accessed: 5 January 2020).

African Union. 2013. *Agenda 2063: The Africa we Want*. Addis Ababa: African Union Commission.

African Union. 2015. *Agenda 2063*. Addis Ababa: African Union.

African Union. 2015. *First ten-year implementation plan 2014–2023*. Addis Ababa: African Union.

Aschauer, David Alan. 1989. "Is public expenditure productive?" *Journal of Monetary Economics* 23(1), 177–200.

Baldwin, John R. and Dixon, Jay. 2008. "Infrastructure Capital: What is it? Where is it? How much of it is there?" *Canadian Productivity Review*. No 16. Ottawa: Statistics Canada.

Ballis, Athanasios, Tsouka, Despoina, Moschovou, T., and Kasselouris, George. 2018. "The Impact of Airport Development on The Tourism in the Greek Islands of the South Aegean Sea," Semantic Scholar. DOI:10.38008/jats.v9i2.25.

Bhatt, V. 2017. Experimental Design for Assessment of Tourism TV Commercials — A case of BRICS. Semantic Scholar. URL: https://www.semantics cholar.org/paper/Experimental-Design-for-Assessment-of-Tourism-TV-%E2 %80%93-Bhatt/7eabe27be73427f9f61d47e731d5bd5cf8f0eeda. Corpus ID: 13854047.

Burke, Michael S. 2020. "The future is now: infrastructure's role in economic recovery," AECOM. URL: https://infrastructure.aecom.com/2020/the-future-is-now-infrastructures-role-in-economic-recovery#:~:text=During (Accessed: 20 November 2020).

Castagnino, Santiago, Subudhi, Suresh, Sogorb, Javier, and Colomar, Pablo. 2020 (September). "The Role of Infrastructure Stimulus in the COVID-19 Recovery and Beyond: Engineering and Construction Industry Response to the Coronavirus," Boston Consulting Group.

Fedderke, Johannes W. and Bogetić, Željko. 2006. "Infrastructure and Growth in South Africa: Direct and Indirect Productivity Impacts of 19 Infrastructure Measures," World Bank Policy Research Working Paper 3989. URL: https://papers.ssrn.com/sol3/papers.cfm?abstract_id=922956 (Accessed: 20 November 2020).

Gartner, Candice. 2016. "The Science and Politics of Infrastructure Research: Asserting Power, Place, and Agency in Infrastructure Knowledge," *Journal of Human Development and Capabilities*, 17(3), 377–396.

Global Infrastructure Index. 2018. "Public satisfaction and priorities — 2018," URL: https://www.ipsos.com/sites/default/files/ct/news/documents/2018-11/ global-infrastructure-index-2018.pdf (Accessed: 5 January 2020).

Jacobs, Bert. 2016. "Can the Addis Ababa Action Agenda Bring about a More Integrated Blend? Facilitating African Infrastructure Development Through Institutionalized Portfolio Approaches," *Forum for Development Studies*, 43(3), 385–413.

Jovanović, Sonya and Ilić, Ivana. 2016. "Infrastructure as Important Determinant of Tourism Development in the Countries of Southeast Europe," *Ecoforum* 5(1), 1–34.

Kay, Cristóbal. 2002. "Why East Asia overtook Latin America: Agrarian reform, industrialization and development," *Third World Quarterly*, 23(6), 1073–1102.

Michael, Noela, Reisinger, Yvette, and Hayes, John 2019. "The UAE's tourism competitiveness: A business perspective," *Tourism Management Perspectives,* 30(1), 53–64.

Palei, Tatyana. 2015. "Assessing the Impact of Infrastructure on Economic Growth and Global Competitiveness," *Procedia Economics and Finance* 23(1), 168–175.

Pradhan, Rudra P., Arvin, Mak B., Bahmani, Sahar, and Norman, Neville R. 2014. "Telecommunications Infrastructure and Economic Growth: Comparative Policy Analysis for the G-20 Developed and Developing Countries," *Journal of Comparative Policy Analysis: Research and Practice*, 16(5), 401–423.

Prud'homme, R., 2005. Infrastructure and Development. Lessons of Experience. *Proceedings of the 2004 Annual Bank Conference on Development Economics*. 153–181.

Sabella, Dario, Serrano, Pablo, Stea, Giovanni, Virdis, Antonio, Tinnirello, Ilenia, Giuliano, Fabrizio, Garlisi, Domenico, Vlacheas, Panagiotis, Pemestichas, Panagiotis, Foteinos, Vasilis, Bartzoudis, Nikolaos, and Payaró, Miquel. 2018. "Designing the 5G network infrastructure: a flexible and reconfigurable architecture based on context and content information," *EURASIP Journal on Wireless Communications and Networking*. DOI: https://doi.org/10.1186/s13638-018-1215-1.

Vindiana, A.P., Novani, S., Mayangsari, L., and Alamanda, D.T. 2020." Analysis of Perceived Factors Affecting Tourist Satisfaction in Mountain Tourism: A Study in Mount Papandayan, Indonesia," *E-Journal of Tourism*, 7(1), 126–137.

# Technology and War

**6**

**Abstract**

This chapter reviews the relationship between technological innovation and the evolution of war. In light of new directions in emerging technologies, primarily AI, and their applicability to war, we present a revision of theoretical outlooks in IR. While the direct applicability of AI in combat is still limited, it nonetheless has a role in strategic analysis. The chapter presents a new model which takes into account the nature of advances being made in automation and additive manufacturing which arguably allow for reduced global interdependence. These threaten the mechanisms which has been a substantial basis of much global peace since WWII. On the other hand, the prevalence of digital platforms for the dissemination for false news will transform much of the rationale for the democratic peace thesis by making information about foreign adversaries less reliable.

**Keywords**: Democratic peace thesis; military R&D; war; war and technology

## 6.1 Introduction

If, as seen in Chapter 5, states are compared in terms of their technological capabilities in infrastructure, it is just as valid that they compare themselves in terms of technology's implications for their security capabilities, and war. Indeed, in our own times, "a metaphorical arms race is in progress in the commercial sphere of autonomous systems development" (Cummings, 2019: 1). Observes Vinod Anand writing for the Indian journal *Strategic Analysis* at the end of the 20th century,

> "Technology has always been used to produce improved tools of warfare. In the modern age, which is normally accepted to have begun after the French Revolution, systematic research in sciences has enabled development of new technology and innovations for both military and civilian use. These have had effects both on the society and the nature of warfare" (Anand, 1999: 137).

Further contemporary analysis by Kumar and Batarseh (2020) determines that "robots that are quicker, stronger, and more accurate will determine who the victor is." It is to be noted that acquisition of new technologies gave advantage not only to European states in their own contests, but also gave them an overall advantage against the various peoples of the New World in Africa, the Americas and Asia that led to their successful colonisation. In modern times, it is the case that a central feature of national security infrastructure entails their capacity to manufacture the most advanced weaponry (Latiff, 2017: 75–76). Indeed, in the United States' total annual military budget of US$600 billion in 2016, some US$200 billion was set aside for research and development as well as procurement of new weapons systems. The US, which has the largest such budget is followed by China, setting the scene for intense geostrategic rivalry with commercial nuances and far-reaching implications (Smith and Browne, 2019: 253). On the other hand, the US' primacy in the global arms sales (measured at US$10 billion in recent years) is seconded by Russia, with whom it accounts for over 50% of the global market (Latiff, 2017: 86). In 2016, the US Department of Defense also formed the Defense Innovation Advisory Board, chaired by former Google CEO and executive chairman Eric Schmidt, along with 11 others selected on the criteria of being individuals with experience in leading large organisations, in both the private and public sectors, and shown excellence in identifying and implementing new technological concepts (Lecher, 2016; Department of Defense, 2016).[1] The role of technology in the evolution of war is well-documented, and as we are witnessing a revolution in technology, observers of military history are also noting the implications of these for military affairs. The leading states' arsenal of weaponry is increasingly composed of new technologies, or newly militarised applications of pre-existing technologies, including lasers, radio-frequency technologies, and autonomous weapons systems based on AI. Importantly and contrary to widely held perceptions, the deployment of autonomous robots in battlefields means soldiers acquiring more responsibilities, not fewer. In the 21st century, nevertheless, war has evolved into

---

[1]In a press statement, Department of Defence spokesperson stated that "the Defence Innovation Advisory Board will seek to advise the department on areas that are deeply familiar to Silicon Valley companies, such as rapid prototyping, iterative product development, complex data analysis in business decision making, the use of mobile and cloud applications, and organizational information sharing" (March 2, 2016).

a barely recognisable phenomenon such that wars of the future will differ both quantitatively and qualitatively from prior conventional conflicts wars according to retired US major general Robert Latiff in his 2017 *Future War* (p. 4). Such a break from the past is the subject of this chapter.

This chapter presents two new theoretical accounts of war in the wake of AI, and one integrative account that combines two literatures. The first unique contribution of the chapter is a hypothesis which states that since inter-state commerce is disrupted by AI and will continue to be, in the wake of widespread automation, the IoT and smart factories, so too will processes of trade interdependence which have kept militancy and war particularly among major powers at bay in the past 70 years of globalisation. In this regard, it is not a coincidence that the relationship between the US and China has been fraught in recent years as both countries' economies have become increasingly automated and AI-dependent. The second is that the democratic peace thesis will require substantial revision in the wake of inaccurate information and thus the information asymmetry problem is of significant importance to scholarship on the democratic peace theory. This is against the US government, through the Pentagon, having published a number of ethical principles of AI in war (Marwala, 2020). In February 2020 the Pentagon unveiled the five ethical principles for AI in warfare, which assume and necessitate a separation of powers, a wide enough pool of responsible expertise with decision making powers. The first of those proposed was the centrality and responsibility of human judgement in AI warfare. The second was ensuring equity through the elimination of bias in AI. The third was ensuring that people understood how AI technology works. The fourth was to ensure that AI systems can be relied upon. The fifth, related to the first, was that humans retain control over AI in order to avoid incidents of unintended harm.

This seems, as all principles and statements of intent tend to be, overly optimistic. How much these will find expression in the incident of a conflict has been the subject of some disagreement, but using the "selectorate"[2]

---

[2]This stems from the concept that every government – whether dictatorial or democratic – rests on a "selectorate" which can include military personnel in the former and the voting-age population in the latter. In turn, decisions are made in consideration of the likely impact on the continued support from such a selectorate. However, the domination of foreign policy decision-making by the military brass has been argued to make military options increasingly of first resort even in democracies (see Ronan Farrow's 2018 book *The War on Peace*).

variant of democratic peace theory, we can propose that a small governing group that tends to be homogenous such as an elite involved in the executive decision making over the deployment of AI indicates that there may be a tendency towards consensus on war as a first policy than on other, more diplomatic routes — more so as AI capabilities in negotiations remain lackluster without convincing proof of concept. Nevertheless, the growth of communicative technologies pave the way for increased public participation. This will likely operate on the basis of information that would be susceptible to manipulation, however. On the other hand, the chapter integrates concepts in mutually assured destruction (MAD) theory with AI capabilities, as it draws a link among works by Bishop and Goldman (2003) and Wilson (2008) in terms of information attacks, which would appear to be relevant to information warfare since by design information attacks, including automated ones, would be aimed at sending enough messages to convince the enemy to unilaterally cease their battle participation (fighting) or indeed to sufficiently disrupt their communication channels such that they are no longer able to counterattack. In the wake of AI, this paves the way for an intensified form of information war that is nonetheless rooted in the policy rationale that war is widely understood to be in the IR scholarship. Thus this chapter looks at the phenomenon of AI in its totality (social, economic and military) to propose modifications to two conventional theories of war.

Section 6.2 describes how AI has been applied in the carrying out of military functions and surveys the R&D landscape in military AI. In Section 6.3 we give an assessment of how technology and warfare have interacted and mutually evolved with one another, and the present state of such a co-evolution. In Section 6.4 we survey the shape of future warfare as indicated in the burgeoning literature on emerging technologies. Section 6.5 provides an assessment of the implications of these transformations for international relations theories and Section 6.6 concludes.

## 6.2　Analysis and Prediction: Mixed Results in AI Applications in War

At its most basic and general form, AI is a technology that looks at how a human brain functions and designing a computer that is able to perform the same functions. As a result, AI programmers are able to create machines that perform well on tasks that humans are able to do, such as in production, as well as analysis and prediction; the latter two being the most directly relevant and thus the focus of this section. AI machines are intelligent, autonomous and able to adapt and evolve beyond the specifications given by their human designers, especially in the wake of machine learning, quantum computing, soft computing and access to Big Data. In this manner, and in many other ways, AI can be dangerous. But the opposite is also true as AI can be beneficial to society. Artificial general intelligence, which is still theoretical at this point, is the capability of AI to execute the same cognition as human beings, without any of the shortfalls of machine learning and thus assume complete responsibility for a variety of functions in governance, diplomacy and military affairs. Given the states of the fields involved, experts suggest that such realities are decades or even centuries away.

Already, artificially intelligent systems are active in analytical roles, where they are involved in sorting large datasets and reaching conclusions on the basis of pattern-recognition; "these are precisely the 'dull' tasks (of the 'dull, dirty and dangerous' formulation) that are generally regarded as the highest priority for automation" (Parakilas *et al.*, 2018: 2). The use of robotics and various other forms of autonomous technologies involved in information-gathering and reconnaissance in warfare has been in place since at least WWII. Many of these early robots (perhaps most notably the American 'Aphrodite' drones in 1944) are deemed to either be not sufficiently effective or to only be useful for specialised operations, with much of the heavy lifting ending up being done by conventional weapons and manned operations. The use of robotics for military operations enjoyed a renaissance and serious consideration and deployment in the 1990s, with the (MQ-1) "Predator" drone being used by the Central Intelligence Agency (CIA) in the Balkans (July–November of 1995) and Afghanistan as part of search efforts to locate al-Qaeda leader Osama bin Laden in September 2000, a year before the 9/11 attacks in New York and the Pentagon, and were further escalated after the attacks.

One of the advantages offered by drones and robotics is distance and remoteness in operations. Rather than meticulously controlling them from close-up radio signals, drones can be controlled through satellites from any location (Kumar and Batarseh, 2020). However, despite the notable progression in making robots ever more intelligent, autonomous robots are still found lacking "the flexibility to react appropriately in unforeseen situations" (Nitsch, 2013; in Kumar and Batarseh, 2020). Thus, contrary to popular perceptions, the deployment of autonomous robots in battlefields means soldiers acquiring more responsibilities, not fewer. Soldiers will still largely be expected to carry out normal military duties and make use of robotics in line with mission requirements (Kumar and Batarseh, 2020).

Indeed, the process of adoption is rather opportunity cost-based, with the pervading consensus being that in order to enjoy full implementation, AI will need to be shown to have similar or greater efficacy as their human counterparts. Put more practically by Parakilas *et al.*, (2018: 5), "if human policymakers are already confident in their human analysts' ability to operationalize a strategically important arms control arrangement, they are unlikely to turn these processes over to a wholly new and unproven system." Overall, then, save by some extraordinary developments, deployment "will not simply be a case of handing over the keys or flipping a switch. There will be no 'artificial analysts' ready to simply take on human roles" and instead AI will undergo incremental pairing with human analysts on specific tasks (Parakilas and Bryce, 2018: 5).

Context greatly aids the incremental pairing process, as recent studies have shown that having context (also termed situational awareness [SA] in militaries) is crucial for intelligent computational agents. Developing and operationalising context for these, however, has proven to be more challenging than the otherwise simpler process of automating repetitive tasks. The key hurdle stems from the difficulty of defining objects which AI has not previously encountered. This is against the impressive performance of human agents who have been able to identify danger from intuition, when "something didn't look right" (Kumar and Batarseh, 2020). Artificial Intelligence, on the other hand, relies on data from past experiences to be able to perceive subtle but important features such as differences in soil textures or a missing equipment. Thus, if an AI agent can offer complementary assistance to soldiers in noticing dangers through contextual data, they can be more effective and useful in battle.

The second role for AI agents is prediction. Placed in this role, "artificially intelligent systems may offer opportunities for policymakers to understand possible future events" (Parakilas and Bryce, 2018: 3). One such modality as identified by Parakilas and Bryce (2018) is in modelling complex negotiations. Additionally, they posit that these can be used in monitoring compliance to international commitments, as well as increasing the capacities of negotiators, while machine-learning methods may be used to forecast others' positions and tactics. This has not been performed so far, however, as limitations persist. In practice, "while predictive algorithms have been demonstrated with some success in some capacities, they are not yet necessarily more accurate than their human equivalents" (p. 3).

On the other hand, scholars have used AI to model the prediction of inter-state conflicts. In their 2011 book, *Militarized Modelling Using Computational Intelligence*, one of this book's authors (Marwala), and co-writer Monica Lagazio developed an AI machine that considered seven factors, also called variables that drive inter-state conflicts. One of these factors is the distance between the two countries' capitals. It turns out that the larger the distance between the capitals of two countries the lesser the likelihood of a war between them. The second variable that is important is whether two countries share a border or not. Countries that share a border are more likely to have conflict. The third factor is the level of trade between two countries. The higher the degree of trade between two countries the less likely is the probability of conflict between these two countries. The fourth factor is the relative difference in the degree of militarisation between two countries. If two countries are equally militarised the probability of war between them is reduced. The fifth is the level of democracy within the dyad, with two democracies never having gone to war. This is the so-called democratic peace thesis.

In this regard, some theoretical revisions on account of the rapid emergence of AI and other relevant technologies in military affairs (particularly relating to variables three and five from the foregoing) in the totality of their societal interface are suggested in the final section of this chapter, which examines the implications for economic interdependence and the democratic peace thesis. In the next section, however, we look at the feedback role of developments in technology and that of war.

## 6.3   Historical Effect of Technology on War

Developments in weapons, communications and transportation have shaped the evolution of warfare. The arrival of gunpowder, wireless radio and armoured vehicles were all decisive factors in their own periods in the change of tactics used in battle. "Nuclear weapons, of course, changed everything" (Latiff, 2017: 65). The significance of nuclear technology will be turned to and discussed in the penultimate section of the chapter. The preceding section discussed some of the more recent innovations and the change in warfare that they ushered in. Notably, however, IR scholars still work based on the insight of Clausewitz that war is nothing but a continuation of policy by other means and thus its outbreak is not substantially affected by arrivals of new technologies. As Bishop and Goldman argue, "even though the repertoire of tools, domains and purveyors of war have changed in important ways, the logic of warfare remains the same" (2003: 114). Then, as ever, war entails the sequencing of attacks with a view to obtain the objectives — which increasingly include interests in the cybersphere — which are driven by political, economic or symbolic objectives. Nonetheless, war is not impervious to technological modernisation and innovation. Though technology may not overhaul or directly alter the underlying policy reasons behind a war, it nonetheless dictates the terms in which it is fought. Consider the following summary from general Latiff (2017: 65–66):

> "[Types of conflicts have evolved from] the "set-piece" battles of the middle ages and the seventeenth and eighteenth centuries and the army-versus-army arrangements of World War I and World War II to guerrilla wars, insurgencies, humanitarian interventions, civil wars, and the global war on terror, with its undefined battlefield and undefined timetable."

In the present context, we are said to be in the paradigm of "fourth generation warfare" (4GW). The concept was first coined by William Lind and his colleagues in the US Marine Corps in 1989 in an article titled "The Changing Face of War: Into the Fourth Generation".

> "In this formulation, first-generation war was characterized by close-order engagements with artillery and massed infantry. Large-scale industrial mobilization, enormous destructive firepower, and tremendous losses defined second-generation war. Third-generation war was all about disruptive tactics, like guerrilla war and sabotage, rather than frontal assaults. Today, fourth-generation war often bypasses military operations altogether, attacking political and cultural targets, employing terror and other criminal tactics" (Latiff, 2017: 66).

Ehrhart (2017: 263) likewise observes that warfare has come into a new, post-modern era of development noting that postmodern warfare constantly moves between war and peace, and shifts between specified geographical nodes in some instances and a lack of defined boundaries in others. This is consistent with 4GW as conceptualised by Lind (2004), who also highlights the element of psychological warfare through doubt. 4GW involves making use of all observed channels, including political, economic, social and military to convey to the enemy's leaders that their strategic goals are not obtainable, and may be costlier than their expected benefit. This is in keeping with the fundamental nature of war which is undergirded by the possession of superior political war which is argued to have the potential to overwhelm even rivals with more economic and military capabilities.

> "4GW does not attempt to win by defeating the enemy's military forces. Instead, combining guerrilla tactics or civil disobedience with the soft networks of social, cultural and economic ties, disinformation campaigns and innovative political activity, it directly attacks the enemy's political will" (Lind, 2014)

However, not all scholars are convinced by the arguments of 4GW. Timothy Junio (2009: 243–244), for example, questions the demarcation of "generations" which he deems as ahistorical and illogical. Where such scholars see neatly demarcated eras, Junio sees biased case selection. In the main, he cites examples of conflicts which took place in prior centuries (and even millennia) which match the characteristics of what 4GW regard as indicative of a new generation. These include guerrilla warfare against Rome, the American Revolution in the 18th century and the Peninsular War in 19th century Spain (Junio, 2009: 243–244).

In a 2005 article, David Sorenson also problematises the paradigm of a 4GW, noting that the notion of a precise shift from one generation to another is flawed, writing that "most of the twentieth-century Middle East wars had elements of both second- and third-generation warfare, so which are they?" (p. 264). Junio echoes this point, stating that at the same time as Mao Zedong's People's Liberation Army (PLA) was conducting guerrilla warfare against the Japanese in China, the war in Europe was being carried out along "third generation" and "fourth generation" tactics, including through direct targeting of civilians in order to diminish morale and undermine political will. "The generations are, therefore, neither logically nor temporally exclusive," he concludes (p. 247). This is problematic in another sense: China was substantially less developed than Europe. In a concept tied to societal evolution, the argument that 4GW began in China and not in the more developed, and inter-state war-prone Europe has this, among many other flaws, to respond to. This is consequential for national security thinking. In policy terms, then, the author dismisses the utility of heeding the advice of 4GW theorists, noting that if lawmakers and the defense officials were to place most of their investment and policy emphasis on 4GW-aimed programs, as advocates of this outlook seem to suggest, it would follow that the decreases in conventional military spending would send a signal to potential adversaries that the prospect of force parity is obtainable (Junio, 2009: 251). Thus, Junio concludes by emphasising the need for infusing this element with the idea of war as evolving in order to be capable of meeting all forms of attacks in the future (Junio, 2009: 251). Rather than one generation supplanting another, other scholars have advanced the notion of an increase in "hybrid warfare", which describes pragmatically engaging in conflict through the use of mixed military and non-military methods as required by the situation at hand (Renz, 2016: 283). Thus, even though they disagree on the precise labels to apply, most security thinkers recognise the shift.

Alongside this evolution, characterised by a growing multiplicity of actors, has been an evolution in technological means and tactics through which policy, to borrow from the influential Clausewitzean formulation,[3] may be expedited. The development of military technology takes the form of a punctuated equilibrium; the status quo persists for a long duration and get interrupted irregularly by new inventions or innovations in application, followed by another duration of no innovation. For example,

> "The introduction of gunpowder and explosives represented a dramatic jump in the lethality of warfare – a discontinuity ... militaries then improved these technologies for centuries, creating bullets, bombs, and cannons. Machine guns and modern artillery may differ in killing power from earlier rifles and cannons, but they are merely improvements to the same technology" (Latiff, 2017: 71).

Likewise, armoured vehicles indicated a major discontinuity in marine warfare. Echoing Diamond (1997) as discussed in Chapter 2, Latiff notes that "military planners at first struggled to figure out how they would be incorporated with mounted infantry and what purpose they would serve." Since then, however, "their utility on the battlefield has repeatedly been proven" (Latiff, 2017: 72). Lastly, innovations in communications have left a long-lasting effect such that today's wars would be impossible to plan without taking into consideration the role of satellites as systems of military command and control rely heavily upon these communications. Interestingly, some four-fifths of military's satellite communications are done through

---

[3] In his influential text *On War*, Prussian military strategist Carl von Clausewitz simplified war as "an act of violence to compel the enemy to fulfil our will" (Von Clausewitz, 1832: 27) and therefore that its tactical specifics are driven by overarching political considerations which remain central even as technologies develop and transform the nature of battles.

commercial systems owned by corporations. Their capabilities could only have been accumulated over time, as they have increasingly surpassed their initial designs:

> "Worldwide monitoring of missile launchers, both tactical and intercontinental, is accompanied by sensitive infrared sensors on board high orbiting systems. They can surveil the entire earth, detect a missile launch, calculate a missile's trajectory, and predict a possible target. They can even make accurate assumptions about the kind of missile based on the heat signature" (Latiff, 2017: 73–74).

These are capabilities that define what humbly began as a system of aiding ships in the open sea (Latiff, 2017: 74).

The onset of new technologies also transforms the course of war. For example, advances in air warfare improved so drastically in the post-Cold War period that Benjamin S. Lambeth, writing in the wake of the Gulf War could postulate that the newly obtained strategic leverage of air power had "unburdened" ground commanders from needing to carry out frontal assaults that require coming into direct contact with rival forces until such a threshold point at which costs associated with such an undertaking would be demonstrable. The major outcome of this, they argued, was that the most important role of land power in high-intensity wars would only be for securing rather than achieving victories (Lambeth, 1997: 66). The elimination of land warfare, however, was an impossibility as it was resisted by related services who have found their interests under sudden threat (Lambeth, 1997: 66). Furthermore, and as a result of this, the private sector is outweighing military investments in R&D. As noted by Davenport (2019), in recent years the total R&D spending of US-headquartered companies Google, Apple, Facebook, IBM, Microsoft and Amazon has been around $54 billion, whilst US Department of Defense (DoD) R&D budget into AI consistently falls short of this, with *Bloomberg* reporting that the US DoD had planned to spend some earmarked US$4 billion in AI and ML from 2020 going forward. High as this number may be, however, it is only about 0.5% of the total budget of the department and less than 10% of the amount spent by large corporations on similar R&D. Elsewhere, Cummings (2019: 1) coheres with this, noting that the gross international defense industry is characterised by the dominance of commercial firms in technological innovation due to the apparent attractiveness of the private sector for talented and highly trained engineers compared to government work.

## 6.4 Trends and Dilemmas in Technology and Warfare

Some scholars have a minimalist view of the magnitude of the changes in technology and what they mean for war. Advancing a minimalist view, Lambeth argued that

> "The list of new air and space technologies that will largely shape future warfare is not long. These technologies are mainly in the areas of projecting power, imposing lethal effects from a safe distance, and enhancing situation awareness. The 'revolution' portended by developments in these three areas will entail changes more in degree than in kind with regard to the nature of individual weapons and support systems. The extent of change it foreshadows for the character of war, however, is decidedly qualitative, because of the newly acquired ability of air and space power to produce decisive results independent of other force elements" (1997: 67).

What is undeniable is the centrality of information; its acquisition, manipulation and management. Future wars will be "heavily dependent on information superiority, and employing strange new weapons" (Latiff, 2017: 5). Moreover, the factor that makes the information age distinct is the prevalence of use of information in war. Crucially, information is useful not only for enhancing the precision of lethal technologies (an already existing use in prior wars), but also for opening up the ability to conduct non-lethal attacks by means of deterring rivals before combat even breaks out. Notably,

> "In important ways, information warfare continues trends that were already underway in the evolution of combat. Like strategic bombing and counter-value nuclear targeting, efforts to deter or defeat an adversary by bypassing destruction of his armed forces and directly attacking his society predate the information technology age. Techniques of information warfare simply provide attackers with a broader array of tools and an ability to target more precisely and by non-lethal means the lifelines upon which advanced societies rely: power grids, phone systems, transportation networks, and [airplane] guidance systems. IT can also make conventional combat more accurate, thereby improving the efficiency of high explosive attacks. Here again, IT continues trends in warfare that have improved the lethality of military force over time" (Bishop and Goldman, 2003: 115).

There is a paradox of vulnerability, however as information technology has rendered most vulnerable those societies which are more advanced.

"Connectivity can increase prosperity and military effectiveness, but it also creates vulnerabilities. Information-intensive military organizations are more vulnerable to information warfare simply because they are more information-dependent, while an adversary need not be information-dependent to disrupt the information lifeline of high-tech forces. Information-dependent societies are also more vulnerable to the infiltration of computer networks, databases and the media, and to attacks on the very linkages upon which modern societies rely to function: communication, financial transaction, transportation and energy resource networks" (Bishop and Goldman, 2003: 116).

On the other hand, the migration to non-confrontational forms of warfare do not rule out the prospect of deployment:

"Despite the characterization of this era as the information age, attacks will surely continue to combine physical and cyber capabilities, as, for example, when IT is used in combined-arms operations to improve the efficiency of high explosive attacks. The means of attack in this case remains predominantly physical. Information simply improves the efficiency and accuracy of physical attack" (Bishop and Goldman, 2003: 118).

As major general Latiff puts it there does persist the possibility of circumstances which will require decision makers to deem it necessary to deploy troops into classic boots-on-the-ground combat situations (Latiff, 2017: 5). Indeed, this has already been the case in US campaigns in Kosovo and the Middle East, whereby the destructiveness of conventional warfare has been enhanced through information technologies in battles (Bishop and Goldman, 2003: 118). Wars have witnessed physical attacks through conventional weapons on command-and-control targets along with non-military infrastructure that nonetheless has military relevance such as electric grids and transportation networks. Some prognoses are less pessimistic, however.

"They could enhance transparency, build confidence and possibly prevent conflict if used in support of arms control verification regimes or peace operations. The increased abilities of sensors to detect military build-ups and disseminate that intelligence could reduce strategic surprise and deter conflict. Information technologies could be used to combat terrorism and international crime through the creation of global databases that track the movements and activities of these transnational actors. Information technologies could possibly prevent genocide and ethnic clashes before they start by ensuring accurate information supplants inflammatory nationalist rhetoric" (Bishop and Goldman, 2003: 120).

Furthermore, the prospect of automated weapons systems is still a future consideration and dilemmas to be brought on by it remain a matter of hypothetical ethical consideration. This is compounded by the fact that autonomous weapons systems and drones are not on the horizon, rendering human involvement a long-term prospective feature of warfare as governments search for the perfect human-machine balance (Gilbert *et al.*, 2018: 206).

## 6.5 Theoretical Implications of Technological Saturation of Warfare

### 6.5.1 *Economic Interdependence*

The first theory we consider to be relevant and impacted upon by the emergence of AI is the concept of interdependence. So far two literatures have formed but have not been connected, this chapter is the first to do so: one has focused on the job losses and structural changes to whole economies that are materialising. The second has seen AI gaining greater application in war, despite current limitations (stemming from difficulties in object recognition that makes them not able to be completely independent in battle as indicated in Section 6.2). The figure indicating the proposed model which integrates the two literatures is represented in Fig. 6.1.

As early as the 18th century, French political philosopher Montesquieu (who in his 1748 work, *The Spirit of the Laws*, argued that "movable wealth" encouraged "peace between and within states"), scholars have advanced the view that "peace is a positive externality of global commerce" (Gartzke *et al.*, 2001: 392). In Book 20 of the same tract, in a chapter titled "Of the Spirit of Commerce," Montesquieu (1748: 346) also went on to further state that peace is the inevitable outcome of trade: "Two nations who traffic with each other become reciprocally dependent; for if one has an interest in buying, the other has an interest in selling: and thus their union is founded on

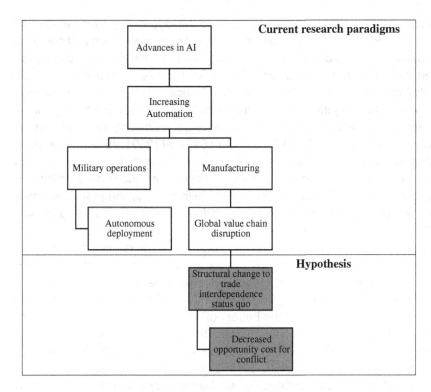

Fig. 6.1.  Proposed automation-trade interdependence status quo disruption.

their mutual necessities." Evidence in recent years appears to validate such observations (D'Anieri, 2013: 65). These studies do indeed link inter-state trade with reductions in militarised disputes or wars among the relevant dyads (D'Anieri, 2013: 72).

Present debates, however, are around *how* precisely the independent variable of trade leads to the outcome variable that is inter-state peace. In 1999 Han Dorussen demonstrated that various trading partners combined with barriers to trade heighten the incentives of states engaging in war or militarised inter-state disputes at the least (Dorussen, 1999: 443). Papayoanou (1999) contends that (given the information asymmetry problem) economic linkages serve the important function of signaling resolve as well as credibility since domestic economic elites in status quo (i.e., pre-war) states come out in support of conflicts which preserve or advance their interests, so the states can be more easily restrained from balancing against revisionist countries with which they have close economic ties (Papayoanou, 1999: 16). Inter-dependence may also affect conflict indirectly through converting state preferences such that countries no longer need to compete with one another. Solingen (1998: 9) for example argues that domestic coalitions (presumably composed of economic elites) who have internationalist economic preferences may create "cross-national bonds" with neighbouring countries and thus forge peace through inter-dependence. State preferences will converge, producing "regional zones of peace" (Solingen, 1998: 9). Finally, Gartzke *et al.* (2001: 391) have asserted that many of the models we have for inter-dependence do not hold up. Namely, since the economic linkages only occasionally deter militarised interstate disputes but run the risk of failing in the long-term, we need a new mechanism of conceptualising their role in discouraging conflict. They thus advance the argument, a la Papayoanou, that inter-dependence presents "nonmilitarized avenues for communicating resolve" by *costly* signaling (Gartzke *et al.*, 2001: 392). In other words, states must be so determined to go to war with the potential adversary that they are willing to forgo the economic benefits currently enjoyed through the economic status quo.

Rise in automation, at the behest of AI, is in the process of re-making the trade patterns which have defined the post-Cold War era of globalisation, and global value chains are undergoing transformation (Charalambous *et al.*, 2019: 1; Prinsloo *et al.*, 2019: 2) which will likely reduce the peace dividend of the present status quo for the majority of the globe. In this way, then, we propose that it will reduce the opportunity cost for initiating conflicts for those states which will be left behind. This section therefore draws a connection which has not been noted; we hypothesise that economic transformation in the wake of AI will disrupt the economic inter-dependence and thus the basis for inter-state peace which has held since the emergence and growth of the present age of globalisation (see Fig. 6.1).

### 6.5.2 *Democratic Peace Thesis*

The democratic peace thesis is particularly affected by the changes which have occurred and are set to occur. A strong variant in the literature argues that domestic political factors explain the relative absence of military violence between democratic states (Marwala and Lagazio, 2011: 3–5). "States sharing republican norms may be more willing to bargain, compromise" well as "[fulfil] contracts than states without these norms" (Owen, 1994: 93–98). Thus whereas neorealism argues that states make war considerations based on capabilities, this variation of the liberal democratic peace thesis argues that the first consideration they make is whether the state they are interacting with is democratic or not. In this regard, liberal states are determined to be more peaceable towards one another because they know themselves to be "reasonable, predictable, and trustworthy" since they are ruled in consideration of the best interests of their citizens. Applied globally, this arguably leads to peace among similarly-run states at it harmonises all individual interests. Liberal democracies are therefore well-positioned to comprehend the intentions behind fellow liberal democracies, as well as the pacific interests which undergird them when dealing with other liberal democracies (Owen, 1994: 95). This grounds some liberal scholars' insistence on a qualified typology of democracies as some democracies may have the formal processes of democracy, but be led by a government that lacks the foundational liberal principles which are argued to make liberal policymakers assume that individuals in the rest of the world are fundamentally similar and therefore best left alone to pursue activities which fulfil the imperatives of material well-being (Owen, 1994: 89). Thus even when war threats are made, illiberal leaders would not be able to "rally the public to fight," or "fear that an unpopular war would lead to their ouster in the next election" (Owen, 1994: 89). Alternately, and possibly where the norms fail to encourage a passive self-restraint on the part of the regime, democratic institutions may constrain leaders from using force against leaders who are likewise constrained (Owen, 1994: 99–101).

According to Bruce Russett (1993: 164), the basis of democratic peace can be broken down into: the monadic proposition and the dyadic proposition. These two propositions are differentiated by the degree of importance they place on the regime type of the targeted state. The monadic proposition is the notion that democratic states are by their nature inclined towards peaceful means of conflict resolution such that they engage in fewer conflicts in general towards democracies and non-democracies (Rummel, 1995: 457). Most quantitative works done on the monadic proposition seem to support the argument. Rummel (1995: 457) therefore argues that democratic societies tend to be more pacific due to the potential ousting of leaders when they lose military campaigns due to the readiness of opposition parties and internal competition within the ruling parties. Others have likewise found that democracies are less inclined to escalate disputes into conventional wars due to the internal structural constrains such rationales pose. According to this structural/institutional model within the monadic perspective, democratic states maintain mutual peace by virtue of constitutional checks and balances that require executives to comply with democratic procedures such as requesting a declaration of war from their legislatures and conducting wars in consideration of tactics which may be in violation of ratified conventions whose disregard requires accountability to court, not to mention civil society (Bueno de Mesquita and Lalman, 1992).

According to the dyadic proposition, on the other hand, democracies are mainly pacific in dyadic interactions (i.e., towards each other) while they are just as likely to engage in war with other regime types (Doyle, 1986: 1161). In opposition to the monadic proposition, this proposition suggests that a crucial determinant is the regime type of the opposing state. Hostility toward non-democratic states is more likely because it is easier to mobilise public support for military actions because non-democratic governments are in states of war with their own populations, which in turn makes their foreign policies incomprehensible to democracies (Doyle, 1986: 1161). Latiff argues that "in the absence of clear and unambiguous public involvement, the military will respond to events in the way it deems most appropriate" (Latiff, 2017: 10). In a group that tends to be homogenous, the literature indicates that there may be consensus on war as a policy of first choice than other diplomatic routes. Nevertheless, the growth of communicative technologies pave the way for increased public participation. This will likely operate on the basis of information that would be susceptible to manipulation, such as when the George W. Bush administration sought to convince the US population — and use as a justification to Congress — the claim that Saddam Hussein's Iraq had weapons of mass destruction and, moreover, was likely to share these with terrorists. As Bishop and Goldman (2003: 115) put it, "we have entered an age where information is not only an adjunct to conventional military and business operations, but has become a key arena of conflict and competition." The tools of information warfare have a tendency to target "enemy population beliefs, enemy leadership beliefs, and the economic and political information systems upon which society relies to function" (Bishop and Goldman, 2003: 119). Figure 6.2 shows the proposed revision to the democratic peace theory in the advent of technological developments. We insert the element of information manipulation through AI such that the domestic audiences may be diverted by their own government, or have their opinion shaped by foreign adversarial governments. The proliferation of AI capable of producing scenes, which can also be strategically disseminated through micro-targeting, poses questions for reliability of the information upon which leaders and, perhaps most importantly, citizens act. Additionally, the elevation of war decisions to a cognitive elite will confine the decision making space. As seen, the conduct of war

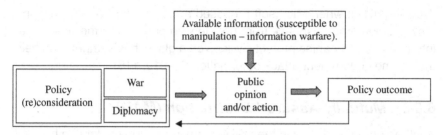

Fig. 6.2. Proposed interaction of democratic peace thesis (constitutional constraints variant) and new technologies. *Source*: Diagram by authors.

has changed from clear territorial (and therefore temporal) demarcations, to less discernable characterisations. The further infusion of AI systems into war will make this increasingly the case, as countries target each other in new and unfamiliar ways. We have already seen, for example, reports of Russian tampering in Estonia's communications systems as well as of Israeli interference in Palestinian waters. This poses another consideration: in instances wherein the population does not feel direct impact of war mobilisation (due to remote campaigns), what means are there for democratic audiences to intervene and cut-off such steps-to-war, including with fellow democracies? In sum, then, adherents of the democratic peace theory need to update the theory to accommodate these new realities.

A wave of global wave protests in 2019 that resulted in the resignations of the national leaders of Bolivia, Iraq and Puerto Rico and a rollback of legislature in Hong Kong put on display that the public is not as complacent as is sometimes portrayed, and at the centre of the coordination methods of the various campaigners was social media. On the other hand, Bishop and Goldman (2003: 120) note optimistically that

> "In democratic nations today, there is a decline in the legitimacy accorded to lethality as well as a redefinition of innocents to include non-military members of an enemy's society. Together, these make anything other than extremely accurate killing increasingly unacceptable in Western societies. The speed and accuracy of information warfare capabilities, coupled with the intolerance of democratic publics for casualties, indiscriminate destruction, and attacks on innocents has raised the attractiveness of this type of information warfare."

Realism, on the other hand, has insights but also encounters dilemmas when the issue of participants is considered. As noted by Smith and

Browne (2019), when Microsoft proposed a "Digital Geneva Convention", they "encountered pushback from people who objected to the notion that international companies protect civilians on a global basis rather than help their home government attack other nations" (2019: 115).

### 6.5.3  *Mutually Assured Destruction (MAD)*

Another long-held theory in the realist paradigm of IR scholarship brought on by technology is mutually assured destruction, that argues that the cost of nuclear attack poses such a threat that no nuclear possessing state is likely to initiate a nuclear war on another. The United States was the first to develop a working nuclear arsenal and to deploy it on Japan in 1945. The US was soon followed by the Soviet Union in 1949, with reports that it managed to do so with secrets stolen from the US.[4] The United Kingdom followed suit in 1952, as did France in 1960 and the People's Republic of China in 1964. These are the only UN-recognised "nuclear weapons states" as they developed these capabilities prior to the opening of the Non-Proliferation Treaty (NPT) for signature in July of 1968 and entry into force two years later. However, some countries abstained from it and were to later develop nuclear capabilities; Israel (1959s), India (1974), South Africa (1970s), Pakistan (1998) and North Korea (2006), being the only country to exit the NPT and subsequently develop nuclear weapons. In the late 1980s, South Africa became the first country to voluntarily dismantle its nuclear arsenal. Others were to follow suit, however as

> "concerns were raised following the collapse of the Soviet Union in 1991, when some former Soviet republics inherited a portion of the Soviet nuclear arsenal. Many experts warned that neither these countries nor a weakened Russia could guarantee the security of their nuclear weapons. Under the Lisbon Protocol (1992), Belarus, Kazakhstan, and Ukraine, as well as Russia and the United States, became parties to the START (Strategic Arms Reduction Talks) treaty between the United States and the former Soviet Union, and the former Soviet republics agreed to destroy or transfer to Russia all strategic nuclear warheads in their territories" (Encyclopædia Britannica, 2019).

---

[4]"Klaus Fuchs, a German-born British physicist who was involved in the Manhattan Project, was later convicted of passing secret information on the theory and design of atomic bombs to the Soviet government" (Encyclopædia Britannica, 2019).

The possession of nuclear weapons by the US and the Soviet Union is said to have been the principal reason behind why the Cold War never materialised into a conventional war and remained a uniquely stable crisis. The role of nuclear deterrence is posited as the foremost reason behind this mutual restraint (see Wilson, 2008: 421; Friedman, 2019: 69). Scholars of MAD emphasise the importance of second strike capabilities; that is, upon being attacked, a state should still be in a position to retaliate with equal or greater force on the initial attacker. Some of these appear to have an overlap with the logics behind escalations in information warfare capabilities. Assessments such as ones outlined in the following, which deploy the concepts of "first strikes" customarily reserved to works on nuclear capabilities, demonstrate as much:

> "Information warfare of [a] disruptive variant is particularly challenging for our understanding of conflict because it blurs the peace–war boundary. Given the technological potential for intrusion, the temptation to pre-emptively disrupt in order to 'prepare the battlefield' before conventional hostilities or a crisis begins, or to incapacitate an adversary's war-making system by causing a complete or partial loss of function, is strong. A pre-battle information suppression operation might shatter an enemy's will to fight but does this first strike constitute a use of force?" (Bishop and Goldman, 2003: 121).

This would appear to be the case as information attacks have the goal of signaling strong messages (either to the leaders or their civilian public, given the necessity of continued political support for war efforts) meant to discourage the rival from further fighting. Functionally, this can also have the benefit of destroying the communications channels available to the adversary for the purposes of military engagement (Bishop and Goldman, 2003: 121–122). In light of the long-standing use of information as a tactic, what we are seeing is a ratcheting up of these pre-existing capabilities. This paves the way for an intensified form of information war that is nonetheless rooted in the policy rationale posited by Clausewitz and from which much of the scholarship has not found substantial evidence to deviate.

## 6.6 Conclusion

In conclusion, we have in this chapter reviewed the utilisation of AI in military conduct, finding that AI has been increasingly used, whilst it is still far from being able to operate autonomously. However, incremental improvements, susceptible to a punctuated equilibrium are still possible, with the private sector at the forefront of research and development in AI with military applications. The broader historical overview implies that technology and war are intertwined, and we may be witnessing a revolution in military affairs, with some military historians, policymakers and security experts debating the timelines and implications. We, however, offer two implications, and in the process indicate the need for revision of standing theories; economic inter-dependence, which we see as being on the verge of transformation with the rise of automation in the production process (and thus the trade status quo), and the democratic peace thesis, with the formation of select epistemic communities, that are susceptible to making decisions towards military more than diplomatic routes, whilst the public may be misguided through the dissemination of information warfare. Thirdly, and in relation to this, we highlight that the process of information warfare may be akin to nuclear warfare, with second-strike capabilities already a priority.

# References

Anand, Vinod. 1999. "Impact of technology on conduct of warfare," *Strategic Analysis*, 23(1), 137–150.

Bishop, Matt and Goldman, Emily. 2003. "The Strategy and Tactics of Information Warfare," *Contemporary Security Policy*, 24(1): 113–139.

Bueno de Mesquita, Bruce and Lalman, David. 1992. "Domestic Opposition and Foreign War," *American Political Science Review*, 84(1): 747–766.

Charalambous, Eleftherios, Feldmann, Robert, Richter, Gérard, and Schmitz, Christoph. 2019 (March). "AI in production: A game changer for manufacturers with heavy assets," McKinsey and Company. URL: https://www.mckinsey.com/business-functions/mckinsey-analytics/our-insights/ai-in-production-a-game-changer-for-manufacturers-with-heavy-assets (Accessed: 3 April 2020).

Cummings, M.L. 2019. "Artificial Intelligence and the Future of Warfare," Chatham House. URL: https://www.chathamhouse.org/sites/default/files/publications/research/2017-01-26-artificial-intelligence-future-warfare-cummings-final.pdf (Accessed: 3 January 2020).

D'Anieri, Paul. 2013. *International Politics: Power and Purpose in Global Affairs* (3rd Edition). Boston, MA: Wadsworth Publishing.

Davenport, Thomas H. 2019. "China is catching up to the US on artificial intelligence research," The Conversation. URL: https://theconversation.com/china-is-catching-up-to-the-us-on-artificial-intelligence-research-112119 (Accessed: 20 November 2020).

Diamond, Jared. 1997. *Guns, Germs and Steel: A Short History of Everybody for the Last 13, 000 Years.* New York: W. W. Norton & Company.

Dorussen, Han. 1999. "Balance of Power Revisited: A Multi-Country Model of Trade and Conflict," *Journal of Peace Research*, 36(4): 443—462.

Doyle, Michael W. 1986. "Liberalism and World Politics," *American Political Science Review*, 80(1): 1151–1169.

Department of Defense [US]. 2016 (March 2). "Statement by Pentagon Press Secretary Peter Cook on the Establishment of the Defense Innovation Advisory Board." URL: https://www.defense.gov/Newsroom/Releases/Release/Article/684201/statement-by-pentagon-press-secretary-peter-cook-on-the-establishment-of-the-de/ (Accessed: 3 January 2020).

Ehrhart, Hans-Georg. 2017. "Postmodern warfare and the blurred boundaries between war and peace," *Defense & Security Analysis*, 33(3), 263–275.

Encyclopædia Britannica. 2019. "Nuclear proliferation," *Encyclopædia Britannica*. URL: https://www.britannica.com/topic/nuclear-proliferation (Accessed: 3 January 2020).

Friedman, Norman. 2019. The Cold War. London: Andre Deutsch.

Gartzke, Erik, Li, Quan, and Boehmer, Charles. 2001. "Investing in the Peace: Economic Interdependence and International Conflict," *International Organization* 55(2), 391–438.

Gilbert, Emily, Adey, Peter, Akhter, Majed, Suchman, Lucy, Wall, Tyler, Weber, Jutta, Parks, Lisa, and Kaplan, Caren. 2018. "Life in the Age of Drone Warfare," *The AAG Review of Books*, 6(3): 206–217.

Hammes, Col., (USMC) Thomas X. 2004. *The Sling and the Stone: On War in the 21st Century*. St Paul, MN: Zenith Press.

Junio, Timothy J. 2009. "Military History and Fourth Generation Warfare," *Journal of Strategic Studies*, 32(2), 243–269.

Kumar, Abhinav and Batarseh, Feras A. 2020 (February 17). "The use of robots and artificial intelligence in war," *London School of Economics Business Review*. URL: https://blogs.lse.ac.uk/businessreview/2020/02/17/the-use-of-robots-and-artificial-intelligence-in-war/ (Accessed: 3 April 2020).

Lambeth, Benjamin S. 1997. "The technology revolution in air warfare," *Survival*, 39(1), 65–83.

Latiff, Robert H. 2017. *Future War: Preparing for the New Global Battlefield*. New York: Knopf.

Lecher, Colin. 2016 (March 2). "Eric Schmidt will chair a Defense Department advisory board," *The Verge*. URL: https://www.theverge.com/2016/3/2/11146884/eric-schmidt-department-of-defense-board-chair (Accessed: 3 January 2020).

Lind, William S. 2004. "Understanding Fourth Generation War," *Military Review* 84(5), 12–16.

Marwala, Tshilidzi. 2020. "South Africa must have a stake in artificial intelligence technology," *Mail & Guardian*. URL: https://mg.co.za/article/2020-03-06-south-africa-must-have-a-stake-in-artificial-intelligence-technology/ (Accessed: 3 April 2020).

Marwala, Tshilidzi and Lagazio, Monica. 2011. *Militarized Conflict Modelling Using Computational Intelligence*. London: Springer-Verlag.

Montesquieu, Charles-Louis (Translated by Thomas Nugent). 1748 [2001]. *The Spirit of the Laws*. Ontario: Botache Books. URL: https://socialsciences. mcmaster.ca/econ/ugcm/3ll3/montesquieu/spiritoflaws.pdf (Accessed 20 March 2021).

Nitsch, Verena. 2013. "Situation Awareness in Autonomous Service Robots," Conference: 10. Berliner Werkstatt Mensch-Maschine-Systeme (October 2013).

Owen, John M. 1994. "How Liberalism Produces Democratic Peace," *International Security*, 19(2): 87–125.

Papayoanou, Paul A. 1999. *Power Ties: Economic Interdependence, Balancing, and War*. Ann Arbor: University of Michigan Press.

Parakilas, Jacob, Bryce, Hannah, Cukier, Kenneth, Roff, Heather, and Cummings, Missy. 2018. *Artificial Intelligence and International Affairs: Disruption Anticipated*. London: Chatham House.

Prinsloo, Jaco, Sinha, Saurabh, and van Solms, Basie. 2019. "A Review of Industry 4.0 Manufacturing Process Security Risks," *Applied Sciences*, 9, 1–31.

Rummel, Rudolph J. 1995. "Democracies are Less Warlike Than Other Regimes," *European Journal of International Relations*, 1(1): 457–479.

Russett, Bruce M. 1993. *Grasping the Democratic Peace: Principles for a Post-Cold War*. Princeton, New Jersey: Princeton University Press.

Smith, Brad and Browne, Carol Ann. 2019. *Tools and Weapons: The Promise and the Peril of the Digital Age*. New York: Penguin Press.

Solingen, Etel. 1998. *Regional Orders at Century's Dawn: Global and Domestic Influences on Grand Strategy*. Princeton, New Jersey: Princeton University Press.

Sorenson, David. 2005. "The Mythology of Fourth-Generation Warfare: A Response to Hammes," *Contemporary Security Policy* 26(2), 264–9.

Wilson, Ward. 2008. "The Myth of Nuclear Deterrence," *Nonproliferation Review*, 15(3): 421–439.

Von Clausewitz, Karl. 1949[1832]. *On War*. London: Routledge and Keagan Paul.

# Technology and Regional Integration

**7**

## Abstract

This chapter reviews the role of technology in regional integration and of regional integration in the development of technologies. Trends are noted in the use of technology to overcome trade barriers, while technologies of exclusion also persist. The chapter also reviews the determinants and the limits of regional cooperation on AI development such as has been seen with the countries of the European Union and extract theoretical insights from these early patterns (particularly neofunctionalism), while also taking stock of the potential limits of the extent to which this model can be applied on a more global scale. We also consider the potential role of China's Belt and Road Initiative in global integration while noting controversies surrounding it.

**Keywords**: European union; regional integration; regionalism; migration; trade

## 7.1 Introduction

While a substantial portion of international interaction is characterised by competitive behaviour, contemporary IR mainly takes the form of cooperation. Particularly explicit among neighbours and states in blocs, regional integration takes many forms and layers but most are unified by their interest in facilitating trade among states in relative vicinity to each other. Overall, there are some 11 regional organisations around the globe. These include the African Union, the European Union, the Intergovernmental Authority on Development (IGAD) in East Africa, the Southern African Development Community (SADC), the Organisation of Islamic Cooperation (OIC), the League of Arab States (LAS), East African Community (EAC), the Economic Community of Central African States (ECCAS), the Gulf Cooperation Council (GCC) and the Association of East Asian Nations (ASEAN), and Southern Common Market (MERCOSUR) in South America.

These groupings pose a challenge for IR theorists and policymakers: do they represent the diminishing role of the state in the international system or do they nonetheless showcase the power of the states, as they operate in an international framework that is shaped by states? Different leaders variously conceive of them as encroachments upon sovereignty or as opportunities to achieve "pooled sovereignty" that allow states to achieve more than they otherwise would on their own (Ndzendze, 2017: 120). Empirical evidence overwhelmingly demonstrates that technology has been co-opted to fulfil both ends — to the result that it intermittently fortifies borders and reduces barriers to access. This has already been the case with AI and other emerging technologies when they interface with regional integration, as we shall see.

In this chapter, we review the role of technology in the growth of regional integration, as well as the role of regional integration in technological development. Technology has proved useful in overcoming conventional barriers to trade. Trends are noted in the use of technology to overcome trade barriers as well as manage migration. The chapter also reviews the determinants and the limits of regional cooperation on AI development such as has been seen with the countries of the EU, while also taking stock of the potential limits of the extent to which this model can be done on a more global scale in other regions. But it is already apparent that the region most likely to influence the pathways and norms around AI and other emerging technologies are to be shaped by the European Union due to its unique blend of technological advancement and external cohesiveness combined with an internally competitive environment.

Section 7.2 discusses regional integration conceptually and theoretically in order to ground the discussion of technology dynamics in regional integration. Section 7.3 discusses the adoption of emerging technologies for managing post-Brexit borders in Europe while Section 7.4 turns to North America. Section 7.5 concludes the chapter with an evaluation of China's Belt and Road Initiative (BRI) as a form of "technological regional integration writ large" while also shining a light on its limitations.

## 7.2  Regional Integration

Regionalism, also termed regional integration, is a process whereby states that share a common defined geographical area pool their resources as well as their polities into some form of cohesive unit. The very definition of what regionalism is immediately indicates some theoretical framework or another; rational choice, liberal internationalism and even geographical explanations. These theoretical frameworks include functionalism, neofunctionalism and intergovernmentalism (Aworaro, 2015: 7). The majority of regional integration measures taken since the 1950s and 1960s have exhibited patterns which most cohere with functionalist and neo-functionalist ideas (Dedeoğlu and Bilener, 2017: 155). The main theory to shed light on globalisation and functionalism, first prominently advanced by Romanian-born British scholar David Mitrany, argued that inter-dependence among states had taken on a life of its own outside regulation and permissiveness granted to them by the states. Rather, functionalists argue, the central actors were individuals and non-state actors and in this process increasingly diminished the relevance of states. As it was later popularised, the essence of his theory was that "form follows function" — the pattern of inter-dependence determines the transnational structures and political bodies which emerge. These ideas are contained in his 1943 book, *A Working Peace System* and several subsequent publications. A problem is encountered for this theory when we look at the slow pace of global integration. In this regard, functionalists have argued that there are impediments to integration in the form of the unwillingness of states to give up their individual sovereignty to a supranational body. Regarding technology, many have argued that while technology serves the function of reducing distances, states have maintained their prominence and indeed served to divide nations (Aworaro, 2015: 7). Encountering such apparent obstacles, these theorists took on a normative turn (making recommendations on what should be done). For example, they posited that for global integration to take place, arrangements ought to start at the levels of social, economic and scientific exchanges with the goal of proving the benefits of such cooperation and indeed their coalescence with states' rational self-interests (Aworaro, 2015: 7). Most prominently, Haas (1957) argued for an approach that was more sectoral and paid attention to individual economic, political and legal components. This approach, he argued, had the benefit of being measurable. Neofunctionalism, on the other hand, adopts the essence and arguments of functionalism but proposes a correction to its level of analysis; while functionalism places greater emphasis on global integration processes, the neofunctionalist school of thought places emphasis on *regional* integration. It is in this sense that the latter has had greater success in helping us understand the manner and pattern of inter-connectedness in the post-WWII period. Regional organisations tend to be more empowered, and, with few notable exceptions,[1] states tend to be more integrated to their regional blocs than to the rest of the world.

There is a spectrum to be highlighted, however. In some instances, states pursue limited regionalism, wherein they formulate trade agreements, and in others they may surrender their sovereignty in one or more areas to carry out specific transactions, in view of achieving an objective or accruing specific benefits to a higher degree than they would on their own; all other things being equal, regional integration results in expanded markets, reduction of costs of doing business, trading and FDI flows (United Nations Economic Commission for Africa, 2016: 45). In addition to enabling innovators to introduce new models of organisation, regional integration leads to novel goods and services, which leads to stimulated productivity (Nicoli, 2020: 897). There is some empirical evidence which demonstrates that there can be negative effects stemming from regional arrangements which take place among unequal states. In these studies, the LDC members are badly positioned and likely to lose out, especially on goods which are homogenous and intramural because they usually have higher trade barriers than their more developed fellow regional arrangement members and thus end up providing greater access to them than they get in return. In a review of North American Free Trade Agreement (NAFTA), for example, Schiff and Wang (2003: 2) argue that the association has caused a static loss for Mexico of some US$3.26 billion (nearly 1% of its GDP) in its early years (Schiff and Wang, 2003: 2).

Regional integration has been advanced as a method for heightening cooperative tendencies among states in the same region, and, where relevant (as in Europe), curtailing militancy and inter-state war by increasing the opportunity cost of instigating conflict by breeding inter-dependency such that any gains to be made from initiating a war with a neighbour would be substantially outweighed by the material loss from the disrupted commerce of the status quo. Regional integration usually takes the form of economic integration, which may then lead to greater political integration. Inevitably, this carries implications for technology, which underlies a great deal of contemporary trade. After World War II, western Europe carried out the largest

---

[1] For example the states of Africa which tend to have an extracontinental trade focus compared to intracontinental, as well as Israel which trades more with states outside the Middle East than within it for political reasons.

such experiment by seeking to link European steel and coal, which were also industries which most readily lent themselves to military technology:

> "European integration began in 1950 with the Schuman Plan, which launched the European Coal and Steel Community (ECSC). The Schuman Plan was designed to alleviate concerns that Germany's dominance in coal and steel could be used to harm European reconstruction efforts or to build another war machine. Jean Monnet, the Plan's chief architect, also wanted to shore up the French planning process for reconstruction by Europeanizing the technocratic planning approach. Most supporters of the ECSC project expected integration to expand beyond Coal and Steel, and hoped that it would serve as a first step toward deeper European integration" (Alter and Steinberg, 2007: 89).

There were suspicions over Germany, the instigator of WWII, which was still the continental leader in steel production. When the ECSC gained approval most observers were concerned that scarcity might play to the advantage of Germany due to the efficient steel industry and high coal reserves in Ruhr. In instances of scarcity, there were thus anxieties that Germany might abuse its dominance and that other European states would be unable to rebuild their own industries and economies more broadly (Alter and Steinberg, 2007: 92). Externally, the ECSC was to also assume the role of being the chief industrial representative of the member states. This was seen, for example, when the US was concerned about dumping of European steel products, and "when a global oversupply led to a collapse of the price of steel products, the ECSC was a useful means to manage the painful but necessary market adjustment" (Alter and Steinberg, 2007: 91). After the Treaty of Rome was signed in 1958, the European Economic Community (EEC), was formed and would evolve into the European Union. The EU came to include more states (who fulfilled the entry criteria including democratisation and certain economic reforms) and assumed more rights, responsibilities and mandates such as law-making for member-states, collective European self-defense and economic policy (with a central bank and common currency used by most of its members, the euro [€], amongst others). The EU is composed of seven main institutions: the European Council, the Council of the European Union, the European Parliament, the European Commission, the Court of Justice, the European Court of Auditors and the European Central Bank. The subject of controversy and criticism, the union has experienced increasing pushback from within some of its member states. This movement, known as Euroscepticism, gained a major victory with Brexit in 2016.

## 7.3  Managing Borders in Europe

In June 2016, the government of the United Kingdom held a referendum in which the public was asked whether their country should stay in the European Union or exit. By a small majority, the people voted to exit, driving the incumbent Prime Minister David Cameron to resign on principle (he had campaigned for continued European Union membership). Among the most salient points touted by those campaigning for Brexit were the restrictions placed on the UK in terms of trade deals, migratory influxes from the continent, the fact that British fishers no longer had an exclusive say over their fishing waters and that the UK made a membership payment which essentially amounted to £300 million per week to the body which could have been useful elsewhere. Less considered was the border between the Republic of Ireland, which is a member of the EU and Britain, through Northern Ireland, which would prove a significant puzzle for the British government. When Britain leaves the European Union, "the border between the north and the south of Ireland will be the only land crossing between the two jurisdictions" (Beall, 2018). However, the history of the border poses a problem, as the British government had committed itself to never putting up a border between the two Irelands, as a method of compromise following the decades-long "Irish Troubles" in a territorial dispute between the government in London and Irish separatist forces. Stuck between wanting to leave the EU and at the same time maintaining the status quo with Ireland on the border, the UK is eager to ensure that a "borderless" arrangement with Ireland qua EU member will not become a conduit for entry into its territory for goods and persons from the rest of the EU, thereby rendering its exit meaningless. The alternative, a "hard border," is not a viable option either: "The problem is, if the UK is out of the customs union, goods coming into Ireland from the UK will have to be checked for compliance with EU standards, tariffs and places of origin, and nobody wants this at the border" (Beall, 2018). Ultimately, it was decided that legally there would be a customs border between Northern Ireland and the Republic of Ireland (ROI) without checks at the border, with checks only on goods that are considered to be "at risk" at "points of entry" into Northern Ireland based on a decision by a joint EU–UK committee (BBC News, 2019). The government of Boris Johnson (coming into office in July 2019) early on insisted that technology could help solve the problem (Beall, 2018). However, this was dismissed as, at least at the time, it was said by at least one observer (Fintan O'Toole, the author of *Heroic Failure: Brexit and the Politics of Pain*) as "a way of minimizing and dismissing an inconvenient truth" (O'Toole, 2019).[2]

Among the proposals, for example, are X-ray scanners which are already installed in many borders, most prominently at the US–Mexico border. These scanners would be particularly useful in detecting dense materials such as bone and metals but would be challenged in their ability to provide clear images of the contents. Another option has been the use of drones. According to a paper by Koslowski and Schulzke (2018: 305), these are also already in use at the US–Mexico border and have been utilised by the EU states albeit for military drones in, for example, patrolling the Mediterranean Sea looking for migrants. But the use of drones is controversial. Particularly it brings a precarious tradeoff between privacy and safety. "First, the encroachment of military technologies into non-military security operations may have adverse security repercussions, but drones may also save migrants' lives as they make dangerous journeys through deserts and across rough seas. Second, drone surveillance erodes privacy but also creates new accountability mechanisms" (Koslowski and Schulzke, 2018: 305).

Thus, while the infrastructure of a hard border may be absent, it may well be nullified by the perceived invasiveness of these hi-tech measures. On the other hand, the lack of feasibility stems from the fact that there are more than 260 roads between Northern Ireland and the Republic of Ireland, which represents more roads than the entirety of the EU Eastern frontier and thus many experts think that there is a limit to how far technology will solve the problem as it cannot be used on every road cost effectively.

These challenges notwithstanding the EU sees itself as a key player in determining the future trajectories and governance of emerging technologies. In its *White Paper on Artificial Intelligence: A European Approach*, the supranational entity posits that "Europe is well-positioned to exercise global leadership in building alliances around shared values and promoting the ethical use of AI" (EU, 2020: 8). Indeed the organisation observes that its

---

[2] As the same author sees it, "using the language of technology to address the questions of history and belonging on the island of Ireland is geeking about memory – like trying to make an algorithm for grief. It's a category error that shunts the problem not just into 'alternative arrangements' but into a parallel universe."

work on artificial intelligence "has already influenced international discussions," such as when its ethical principles were adopted by the 37-member OECD and the G20 in June 2019 (EU, 2020: 8). To varying degrees, these ethical principles will, in turn, be internally adopted by numerous countries. In this sense, the emerging technologies are cohering with neofunctionalism: the regional organisation is the first mover. Although some originated in the domestic settings of Germany (due to the work of its Data Ethics Commission), Denmark (from its Data Ethics Seal) and Malta (from its voluntary certification system for AI), they have received refinement and universal application through the regional entity. The EU has also set up standards for R&D, skills development, support for small and medium enterprises, modalities for partnership with the private sector and promoting AI uptake in the public sector (EU, 2020: 8). In addition to neofunctionalism, the pathway for AI ethics is likely to take an inter-regional character as the EU heeds insights from work of other international organisations such as the UNESCO and the World Trade Organization (WTO). At the UN, the EU is a key participant in the Follow-up Report of the High-Level Panel on Digital Cooperation, whose recommendations reflect EU positions (EU, 2020: 8).

## 7.4   North America: The US–Mexico Border

Regions are more than their economic sinews, there are also popular and cultural considerations at play. It is through these lenses that the ultimate ends of technologies are people. Even in a context of flourishing commercial ties, political integration may lag behind. A commonly cited example is that of the US–Mexico border. In spite of increasingly stringent border security requirements, "North America is a vibrant and active region that continues to have high flows of vehicles, trucks, and persons across the borders shared with Canada and Mexico" (Chavez and Hoewe, 2010: 182). At the core of this has been the North American Free Trade Agreement. Since the establishing of NAFTA, US–Mexican trade has grown from US$297 billion in 1994 to US$677.3 billion in 2019 — or a shift from US$813 million to US$1.855 billion traded per day. This represents a growth rate of 213%. Overall, the regional arrangement proved impervious even to the 2008/2009 Great Recession and grew to over US$1.1 trillion (Chavez and Hoewe, 2010: 182). But this focus on economics downplays some issues below the surface. On the US side, there is dissatisfaction over manufacturing jobs moving to low-wage Mexico, while on the Mexican side, there are concerns over safety in those factories. The US also had complaints about Canadian government's subsidies to its agricultural industry (particularly dairy) which made it difficult for the US to compete, its own agricultural subsidisation notwithstanding. In 2018, the US's efforts to reverse NAFTA succeeded when the leaders of the three countries signed the new United States-Mexico-Canada Agreement (USMCA). Canadian businesses worry that the lack of data protections leaves Canadians vulnerable to being "data mines" for US Big Tech corporations. "We are cascading toward a surveillance state," commented Jim Balsillie (the co-founder of Research in Motion (RIM) which used to produce the BlackBerry smartphones) in a hearing. For its part, the Canadian government, under Prime Minister Justin Trudeau (who had undertaken a special trip to Silicon Valley a year before), appeared eager to sign the deal with the hopes of consolidating commercial relations with the US and attracting American companies to set up in the country (Barth, 2020). Matters are seen differently in the country south of the US border. Part of the revisions on the USMCA includes the requirement for a minimum wage of US$16/hour in manufacturing. This is seen as a US effort to eliminate Mexico's comparative advantage in low-cost labour which had led to US companies being attracted to Mexico. This was negatively received in Mexico. But such discontent was nothing new.

As the United States puts in place more stringent measures aimed at securing its border with Mexico, the perception of the US by Mexico has been largely negative (Chavez and Hoewe, 2010: 181). Even in spite of Mexico's strategic importance, the area of public diplomacy has not been particularly explored by the US, particularly on the border — even before the ascendence of Donald Trump to the US presidency. In the early Obama administration, Chavez and Hoewe (2010: 181) had suggested that "the United States ought to utilize technological resources to encourage com-munication facilitating public diplomacy with Mexico. In this way, the United States could lessen the negative public opinion of it throughout Mexico." It is the view of these scholars that the United States has done little to improve these relations.

"Despite ample technological resources to host discussions, the country has ignored the role of public diplomacy in addressing U.S.-Mexico border relations. Overall, public diplomacy has been used mainly to foster government relationships and policy devel-opment but has been largely neglected at the border level. The United States ought utilize technological resources to encour-age communication facilitating public diplomacy among North American countries, specifically Mexico" (Chavez and Hoewe, 2010: 187).

The North American version of regional integration appears to exhibit inter-governmentalism more than the pattern of neofunctionalism observed in Europe. In light of this, the authors suggest that making use of social media platforms can aid the US to diminish negative perceptions held over the US in Mexico. This is a strategy they deem feasible due to high Internet penetration and widespread use of social media platforms in Mexico. They are advocating for the use of social media for strategic communications through which, at the very least, the US can articulate the rationale behind its policies pertaining to the border (Chavez and Hoewe, 2010: 188). They propose, in particular, that "making this information widely available in simple language may help ease the tension created by controversial policy decisions involving the US–Mexico border. Government operations, such as the Office for Innovative Engagement, provide the ideal setting to test and, ultimately, put to use this approach to public diplomacy" (Chavez and Hoewe, 2010: 188).

The authors also suggest online and TV adverts that would advocate for open information along with friendly hashtags. Were it written today, the paper would perhaps argue for use of Big Data and AI to detect themes which would have the most relevance as well as guide the deployment of such strategic communications along specific temporal and spatial dimensions. These would, especially if availed in English and Spanish, "be more attractive to the Mexican audience" than exclusively English language broadcasts (Chavez and Hoewe, 2010: 188). Finally, the suggestion would provide a platform for the target audience to voice concerns about policy and forge a direct line of communication for both sides and forge grassroots public diplomacy. This strategy has been used by numerous other countries as virtually every country has a social media account. This has proved especially useful in the face of COVID-19, a period of uncertainty. AI offers the opportunity to do these communications smarter and with more precision. Advances are being made in the private sector. We briefly discuss this in the following.

As a response to the international migration crisis, independent Zimbabwean programmers have developed a method of predicting the next refugee crisis with the use of AI (Hakizimana, 2019: 128). The methodology utilises algorithms drawn from historic World Bank derived data so as to identify patterns exhibited in prior crises and detects whether the variables that led up to the previous crises correlate in any form with a given situation at hand. These variables include the food production index, GDP statistics, weather forecasts, as well as data on climate change and political reports (Hakizimana, 2020: 128). Thus experts can predict the likely time of the next ensuing crisis and be able to prepare the public in advance so that the number of displaced people due to the crisis is mitigated or at least anticipated (Hakizimana, 2020: 128). This solution is not perfect due to a 10 to 15% margin of error being exhibited by the algorithm. Moreover, it has been observed that the fact of the predictions being entirely reliant on data points that were, for the most part, captured by human beings makes the algorithm liable to human error. Moreover, the determinants of successive crises are not identical to each other (Hakizimana, 2020: 128). Also, many national statistical offices have limited resources and are thus unable to conduct frequent surveys that allow them to measure changing trends over time.

As AI and other emerging technologies improve, they will gain ever-increasing use in the integration of countries and regions. But as we have seen in both the cases of the EU and North America, technology can just as well be an instrument of ensuring digital fortresses depending on the political and economic climate.

## 7.5 Integration and Technology Writ Large? China's Belt and Road Initiative

The BRI was first announced in 2013 by Chinese President Xi Jinping, then in his second year in office, during a state visit in Kazakhstan. The plan is comprised of two multipronged infrastructurally-based trade routes, by land (the Economic Belt) and by sea (the Maritime Silk Road), (tacitly or openly) acceded to by more than 70 countries at the time of writing. On paper, the BRI is the largest economic project the world has ever seen from a single country. Manuel notes that the scope of the BRI could see some $1 trillion being spent by 2027 (Manuel, 2017: 1).

The implications of this for the global economy, and by extension for global politics, are still to unfold and therefore yet to be unpacked. But it falls within the arch of Chinese foreign policy since 1978 with the Reform and Opening Up policies under Deng Xiaoping, and most recently within the trajectory set in motion since 2001; and in that regard, we can distil some patterns and reach some early conclusions. In that year, China adopted the "Going Out" Strategy that encouraged Chinese firms to participate in cross-border investment. Since then, Chinese OFDI has been increasing rapidly, reaching US$118 billion by 2015. As the third-largest FDI source nation globally and at the same time a developing country, China arguably bears different characteristics when it comes to the motivation and risk attitude of its foreign investment (Liu *et al.*, 2017: 1374). From the Chinese point of argument, at the centre of the combined concepts collectively known as the BRI is the idea of "shared prosperity," with linkages of China with Africa, Europe, the Middle East, Central Asia and South Asia (and these entities to each other). This implies a kind of regionalism writ large through technology.

While "One Belt One Road" (or OBOR, its original name when it was announced) implied only a single network, the Chinese government's aim in renaming the initiative to the Belt and Road Initiative has been rooted in hopes that the latter etymology would "better reflect the project's numerous network cluster," and "would also make it sound more like an inclusive initiative rather than a strategy, echoing Xi's claims that 'the "Belt and Road Initiative" is not set by ideology' or 'a political agenda'" (Zhu, 2020: 6). However, the attendance by only 29 world leaders at the (May 14–15) Belt and Road Forum marking the official launch of the BRI in early 2017 raised doubts about the commitment of the then 65 countries that were involved in the New Silk Road. Notably, the list excluded regional powers such as India and Japan, who had been having deep, long-standing and geopolitically-rooted concerns about the implications of what they perceived as China's economic expansion. Indeed one of the most important nodes of the BRI, the China-Pakistan Economic Corridor (CPEC), traverses through territory under dispute between India and Pakistan. Tokyo and New Delhi instead later unveiled that they been working on an "alternative Belt and Road Initiative" of their own, named the Asia-Africa Growth Corridor (AAGC), announced at the 2017 African Development Bank's annual general meeting held in India, just weeks after the Belt and Road Forum. More than a few of the participating countries, some of which were European (including France, Switzerland and Spain), arguably retained some reservations regarding China's mega initiative. At the core of the reservations are fears that the initiative is less about philanthropy and more about hard power. Stanzel (2017: 1) observes that contrary to China's official claims of the initiative being benign, the BRI is increasingly interpreted as a geopolitical and geoeconomic strategy. Others have likewise noted a militaristic undertone to the BRI. Johnson and Luce (2018) argue that China's acquisition of more than 12 ports across the Indian Ocean appears to be a Beijing-driven plan to shore up China's political and military presence from Indonesia and East Africa (Johnson and Luce, 2018).

Perhaps fueling the speculation has been the information deficit in the early days of the initiative. Grossman (2017: 1) observes that the BRI set off a spectrum of reactions, mainly due to the scantiness of details on the grand initiative. "While the stated goal of the BRI, otherwise termed OBOR, is to expand ties between Asia, Africa and Europe across a range of sectors, uncertainty about the precise aims and impact of the policy remain." Johnson and Luce (2018) further add that "the economics of the deals are questionable, political control is nearly absolute, and one of the main drivers is to give the Chinese navy the possibility of far-reaching logistical support under the cover of seemingly innocuous commercial operations." For its part, and perhaps expectably, Beijing has maintained that it is committed to taking an inclusive approach to trade and diplomacy through the BRI, with Xi Jinping (2018: 42) writing in *The Governance of China II* that:

> "China is committed to an independent foreign policy of peace and developing friendly cooperation with all other countries on the basis of the Five Principles of Peaceful Coexistence. China follows the basic state policy of opening up, developing its economy with the door open to the outside world. Through major international cooperation projects like the Belt and Road Initiative, we work to create a more comprehensive, diversified and deeper opening-up structure."

This view, consistent with iterations by previous Chinese leaders as far back as Mao Zedong, can hardly be convincing to countries that see Beijing in nefarious terms. On the other hand, the BRI cannot operate without trust by the countries with whom China hopes to gain cooperation. Issues working against China are mistrust by governments and civil society in the developed world over Chinese technology, as well as mistrust by segments of populations in developing countries over the prospect of perpetual indebtedness to China. In this regard, the coronavirus pandemic may play a catalytic role and to possible mutual advantage, though this is not guaranteed, as other countries look to stimulate their economies through infrastructural inputs and move into 4IR technologies. But the central problem of the BRI would appear to be its excessive inter-governmentalism. So far, China has sought to have it both ways: presenting the BRI as a universal aspiration while still maintaining control over it and its meaning and pathways. The success of neofunctionalism ought to illustrate that the initiative will ultimately succeed not on the basis of governmental pushes but on the back of its adoption by non-state actors.

## References

Alter, Karen J. and Steinberg, David. 2007. "The Theory and Reality of the European Coal and Steel Community," in S. Meunier and K. McNamara (Eds), *Making History: European Integration and Institutional Change at Fifty*, pp. 89–104. Oxford: Oxford University Press.

Aworaro, Friday. 2015. "Regional integration and development in Africa: Between the present realities and overcoming future challenges," *African Journal of Governance and Development*, 4(2), 5–16.

Barth, Brian J. 2020. "Are You Afraid of Google? BlackBerry Cofounder Jim Balsillie Says You Should Be," *The Walrus*. URL: https://thewalrus.ca/are-you-afraid-of-google-blackberry-cofounder-jim-balsillie-says-you-should-be/ (Accessed: 22 November 2020).

BBC News. 2019. "Brexit: What is in Boris Johnson's new deal with the EU?," BBC News. URL: https://www.bbc.com/news/uk-50083026 (Accessed: 3 November 2020).

Beall, Abigail. 2018 (June 1). "As Brexit looms, it's clear the tech to solve the Irish border problem is either untested or imaginary," *Wired*. URL: https://www.wired.co.uk/article/irish-border-brexit-tech (Accessed: 3 January 2020).

Chavez, Manuel and Hoewe, Jennifer. 2010. "Reconstructing public diplomacy in the context of policy, communication, and technology: An examination of U.S. - Mexico border relations," *Journal of Borderlands Studies*, 25(3-4), 181–190.

Dedeoğlu, Beril and Bilener, Tolga. 2017. "Neo-Functionalist Regional Integration Theory Put to Test in Asia," *Insight Turkey*, 19(4), 155–174.

European Union. 2020. *On Artificial Intelligence - A European approach to Excellence and Trust*. White Paper. Brussels: European Commission.

Grossman, G. 2017. *One Belt, One Road and the Sino-Mongolian Relationship*. Berlin, Germany: Stiftung Asienhaus.

Haas, Ernst. 1957. "Regional Integration and National Policy," *International Conciliation*, No. 513 (May).

Hakizimana, Nadine. 2019. *Intellectual Property and Regional Trade in the Southern African Development Community*. Masters Thesis: University of the Witwatersrand, Johannesburg.

Johnson, K. and Luce, D. 2018 (April). "One Belt, One Road, One Happy Chinese Navy," *Foreign Policy*. URL: https://foreignpolicy.com/2018/04/17/one-belt-one-road-one-happy-chinese-navy/ (Accessed 3 January 2020).

Koslowski, Rey and Schulzke, Marcus. 2018. "Drones Along Borders: Border Security UAVs in the United States and the European Union," *International Studies Perspectives*, 19(4), 305–324.

Manuel, Anja. 2017 (October 17). "China Is Quietly Reshaping the World," *The Atlantic.* URL: https://www.theatlantic.com/international/archive/2017/10/china-belt-and-road/542667/ (Accessed: 20 November 2020).

Ndzendze, Bhaso. 2017. *Beginner's Dictionary of Contemporary International Relations.* NLSA: Pretoria.

Nicoli, Francesco. 2020. "Neofunctionalism revisited: integration theory and varieties of outcomes in the Eurocrisis," *Journal of European Integration,* 42(7), 897–916.

O'Toole, Fintan. 2019. "The Irish border is a matter of life and death, not technology," *The Guardian.* URL: https://www.theguardian.com/commentisfree/2019/oct/08/brexit-irish-border-technology (Accessed: 3 January 2020).

Schiff, Maurice and Wang, Yanling. 2003. "Regional Integration and Technology Diffusion: The Case of the North America Free Trade Agreement," Policy Research Working Paper No. 3132. The World Bank.

Stanzel, Angela. 2017. "China's Belt and Road – new name, same doubts?", *European Council on Foreign Relations,* URL: http://www.ecfr.eu/article/commentary_chinas_belt_and_road_new_name_same_doubts# (Accessed: 5 January 2020).

Xi, Jinping. 2018. *The Governance of China II.* Beijing: Foreign Languages Press.

Zhu, M. 2020. "BRI Space Information Corridor and its roles in SDGs. Shanghai, China," Shanghai Institute of International Studies.

# Diplomatic Engagement and Technology

# 8

**Abstract**

This chapter explores the dual relevancies of technology to diplomatic engagement; that is, technologies as both the subject and catalysts of bilateral and multilateral interactions. The former is explored in the first section, and the latter in the second. Both are conducted with empirical cases. In the third section, the chapter seeks to highlight the encroachment of the "Westphalian" monopoly of states on the international diplomatic stage in light of the growing number of actors involved in responding to new challenges brought on by the development of emerging technologies, particularly nuclear proliferation, climate change and e-waste management. Additionally, it ponders the diplomatic implications of AI and other emerging technologies.

**Keywords**: Digital geneva convention; diplomacy; proliferation; sovereignty

## 8.1 Introduction

"Diplomacy," observes Olubukola Adesina, is "the established method by which states articulate their foreign policy objectives and co-ordinate their efforts to influence the decisions and behaviour of foreign governments and peoples through dialogue, negotiations and other such measures, short of war and violence" (Adesina, 2017: 3). Many of the topics covered in this book now require dialogue and negotiations in order to avert such violent outcomes. In other words, diplomacy, a concept with a history that stretches thousands of years, will need to become ever more cognisant of the threats and opportunities posed by the emerging technologies discussed here. National interests and global sustainability are under strain. This is increasingly being recognised. Such is the growing centrality of technology to diplomatic endeavours that in its 2019 *Foreign Policy Review*, the South African Department of International Relations and Cooperation

(DIRCO) notes that the "usage of modern technologies must be part of DIRCO's efforts to reclaim leadership role on the [African] continent and repositioning the country as an important player in global affairs" (Department of International Relations and Cooperation (South Africa), 2019: 39). It is fitting to have the final chapter on diplomatic engagement as it relates (and will further relate) to technology.

From the emergence of WikiLeaks, to the reported interference in the 2016 US elections, to proposals of a "Digital Geneva Convention", new forms of technologies are increasingly thrusting into the public sphere matters of diplomacy, war and security. Although diplomacy's conventional role (i.e., "interactions between representatives of sovereign states" [Adesina, 2017: 2]) maintains its purpose, in today's extraordinarily interconnected world non-state actors have a major to play role in global affairs. Bousfield presents findings which demonstrate that there has been unprecedented citizen-to-citizen interaction alongside ministerial and ambassadorial relations (Bousfield, 2017: 1048). This is the so-called digital diplomacy (sometimes also termed e-diplomacy), part of which was discussed in the preceding chapter in our consideration of use of social media in US–Mexican relations. It leads to greater flows of information, interaction and transparency among states but also contains risks through anonymity, hacking and instantaneous communication without sufficient communication. These are arguably outweighed by the benefits, however (Rashica, 2018: 75). They will also become ever more needed in the age of AI.

This chapter explores the dual relevancies of technology to diplomatic engagement. It posits technology as both the subject and a catalyst of foreign policies in bilateral and multilateral contexts. The former is explored in Section 8.2, and the latter Section 8.3. Additionally, in Section 8.4, the chapter seeks to highlight the encroachment upon the "Westphalian" monopoly of states on the international diplomatic stage in light of the growing number of actors involved in responding to new challenges brought on by the development of technologies, particularly nuclear proliferation, climate change and the growing issue of e-waste management which has been a byproduct of the centuries-long innovation described in the seven preceding chapters.

## 8.2   Science and Technology Diplomacy

Initially dominated by a "libertarian" point of view that advocated for limited oversight and involvement in setting regulations in the early 1990s, this hands-off approach towards regulation of the Internet was soon displaced by international legal scholars who asserted that international regulation of the Internet was both feasible and legitimate (Serrano, 2019: 1). By 2010, a United Nations background paper on fighting online criminals was referring to cyberspace as "the fifth common space — after land, sea, air, and outer space" (Schjolberg, 2010: 1). This is justifiable given that the Internet has become a space wherein people and groups live, socialise and manage their finances among other functions which rely on sensitive data (Moore, 2017: 1). Today's International Telecommunications Union (ITU), which is the custodian of the international governance of the Internet, has two predecessor institutions. The first was the outcome of decades-long diplomatic efforts and agreements between 1849 and 1865 in order to generate homogenous standards. In 1865 (1 March to 17 May) the French government hosted a series of conferences that were attended by delegations from 20 European states. This resulted in the International Telegraph Convention, which codified the adoption of Morse code as the alphabet of the telegraph, international rights to telegraphic communication and the right to secrecy in such communications. Some 41 years later, in 1906, yet another innovation required international cooperation. This was the radio. By then hosted in Berlin, Germany, the talks, which were attended by 29 nations, resulted in the International Radiotelegraph Union. In 1932, the two bodies were merged into the ITU, incorporating provisions for telephones as well. In September 1947, the ITU entered into discussions with the United Nations to become one of its specialised technical agencies. This was finalised and made official on New Year's Day of 1949. The work of the ITU is crucial. It has sustained its role in ensuring the shared global use of the radio spectrum (in the electromagnetic spectrum from 9 kHz to 275 GHz), globally oversees TV broadcasting, forges global cooperation in space exploration through assigning satellite orbits, assists in generating and implementing technical standards on a worldwide scale, and is at the forefront of improving telecommunication infrastructure in the low and middle income states. One of its more recent efforts has been to bridge the divide in digital access under the auspices of the World Summit on the Information Society (WSIS) convened in 2003 and 2005, which has since become a standing body.

In contemporary terms, technology as a subject of diplomacy is noted most pointedly in science and technology diplomacy. For the receiving countries, this form of diplomacy is an additional avenue for technology transfers (in addition to trade and FDI as covered in Chapter 3) and policy adaption. In a policy document co-authored with the English Royal Society, the authors observed that "[a]dvances in science have long relied on international flows of people and ideas" (Royal Society, 2010: v). In 1963, the United Nations organised the Conference on the Application of Science and Technology for the Benefit of Less Developed Areas, which was the first such conference on a global scale by the UN focused on science and technology as useful and important tools for development. It was based on the premise that the developing countries could "leapfrog" and reach generations of innovation within a short space of time by taking up technologies from industrialised countries. The conference led to a multipronged approach to providing science and technology advice (United Nations Conference on Trade and Development (UNCTAD), 2003: 7). Elements of this key insight were incorporated into the Millennial Development Goals (MDGs) and latterly the SDGs. The benefits for the developing states are self-evident.

For the transferring states, on the other hand, science diplomacy allows them to supplement its foreign policy credentials. Increasingly, science and technology diplomacy are major concepts in many countries' soft-power arsenals. Soft power refers to the concept that states can gain prominence either through coercive means such as military strength (hard power) or through persuasiveness by cultivating a good image of friendliness that other states want to be associated with or benefit from. In practice of this in Asia and Africa, pre-Great Recession Japan contributed through hydraulic engineering projects and public works programmes such as facilitating sewage systems, building or refurbishing ports, installing irrigation systems, as well as providing agricultural and medical assistance from its own public purse (Yakushiji, 2009: 1). This comes from a recognition that today's poor and underdeveloped countries lack in precisely those features which developed countries such as Japan particularly excel the most. This also presents Japanese scientists with the opportunity to expand their expertise in new and unfamiliar environments:

> "[D]ue to the globalization of science and technology, Japanese scientists and technologists now enjoy greater working opportunities in the international arena than ever. As well as being first-rate scientists and technologists, they could also be described as private envoys representing Japan."

The benefits for the Japanese government are also clear according to Taizo Yakushiji:

"They put down roots in local communities, become friends with their local colleagues and other people, and make progress in their research. From a different perspective, their activities could even be said to typify Japan's superb diplomatic human resources. In a sense the new expression "science and technology diplomacy" has served to create new human resources on both the diplomatic and the science and technology sides of the fence" (Yakushiji, 2009: 2).

A related example is South Africa after 1994. In a white paper published in 1996, South Africa's first democratic government emphatically stressed the major role that could be played by science and technology as means of economic growth and poverty alleviation (Pandor, 2012). According to the country's erstwhile Minister of Science and Technology, Naledi Pandor, this carried significance as a way to reverse the effects of the isolation experienced during the sanctions era of the late apartheid period and to allow the country to develop, for the first time, relations with fellow African countries. It also presented an opportunity to take advantage of international partnerships to fulfil national programmes, foremost among which is capacity building (Pandor, 2012). Leadership in science diplomacy may also be a statement of prowess by emerging powers. Particularly in the case of China, a 2018-published multi-country study by the University of Southern California Center on Public Diplomacy finds the following:

"Initially, China engaged with the international community by sending Chinese students to Western universities, competitively pursuing joint scientific work and publications among young academics, maintaining relations with the growing Chinese scientific diaspora abroad, and by developing national science and technology parks. China's signing of international agreements was testimony to its openness to cooperation and marked China's entrance onto the world stage" (Krasnyak, 2018; December 13).

The preceding examples have discussed relationships between technologically asymmetric states providing opportunities to one another. But parity is also possible. Countries in relatively similar stages of development can benefit from tapping into each other's mutual areas of comparative advantage. It also paves the way and creates a platform for multilateral engagement on global issues. Indeed, for the United Nations, the term science and technology diplomacy refers to "the provision of science and technology advice to multilateral negotiations and the implementation of the results of such negotiations at the national level. It therefore covers activities at both the international level and national level pursuant to international commitments" (2003: 3). At the same time, however, there is a balance to be established on nationally sensitive technologies whose internationalisation may border on encroachment. This concept is explored more fully in the final section of this chapter.

In keeping with the non-state and sub-state theme, a trend is emerging whereby cities, as major economic and innovation players are gradually transforming the international arena and thereby bypassing their nation-states to the extent of creating what is being labelled city-centred international relations (Roig, 2018; emphasis added). In this regard, Barcelona, the regional capital of Catalonia in Spain, is a notable leader. The city plays host to hundreds of consulates and ranks fourth in the world in terms of non-state foreign offices. Among these are headquarters of the 42-member and intercontinental Union for the Mediterranean which includes European, African and Middle Eastern countries; the regional offices of the WHO; the UN-HABITAT City Resilience Profiling Programme; and the Global University Network for Innovation. A trend is emerging whereby as cities aspire to become smart cities, they have increasingly taken charge of various aspects of foreign policy.

The remainder of the chapter proceeds with a review of technology as a catalyst in foreign policy objectives and concludes by assessing emerging global issues that have amassed and are increasingly amassing global diplomatic participation.

## 8.3   Technology as a Diplomatic Catalyst

Diplomacy and technology intersect most notably in terms of intelligence gathering. Embassies function as intelligence bases and as such can be, and have been, key sites for intelligence attacks in their host countries (Herman, 1998: 1). However, the relationship is not a clearly demarcated one and as a result the two sectors are undergirded by competition such that intelligence has come to be described as essentially anti-diplomacy. In prior centuries, diplomats had the additional role of managing secret operations that entailed information-gathering. Leaders of countries had as part of their work the review of intelligence reports in this unspecialised sector. This method had an inherent drawback which sowed the seeds of its own demise; it was not institutionalised and as such was *ad hoc* and could thus not be relied upon by the armies and navies that required quality intelligence in times of war. A transformation thus occurred in the mid-1800s, at the root of which were new applications of the technologies gained through the successive industrial epochs:

"The new technologies of the industrial revolution produced new forms of war, in which armies and navies needed pre-planning based on stores of information about potential enemies and their railways and topography. Permanent military and naval intelligence departments were established in Britain in the 1870s and 1880s and in America in the 1880s; rather earlier in continental countries. At first these did not impinge on diplomacy's position. Embassies provided information on foreign forces through their military and naval attaches" (Herman, 1998: 2).

Nonetheless, secret intelligence continued to see growth in the late 19th century and the beginnings of the 20th century, as states were becoming more vigilant over their national secrets (Herman, 1998: 3). Ideological stratification after WWI and the communist revolution in Russia subsequently heightened these fears and increased the premium states placed on countering espionage, especially as there were mutual suspicions due to the recent memory of the overthrow of the centuries-old Russian monarchy, and the infancy and potentially tenuous victory for the Bolsheviks; this ensured the peace-time maintenance of intelligence apparatus for states (Herman, 1998: 3). WWI — as the first "total war" of the industrial age — coincided with technological sophistication, particularly relevant were radio interception and signals intelligence. There was also the application of airborne photography for reconnaissance operations. As a result of this, WWII, which took place 20 years later, was to be "even more [of] an intelligence war, particularly with the scale of Western successes in breaking enemy ciphers," and "the early years of the Cold War then saw intelligence collection develop on a quite unprecedented peacetime scale, even further increased by the introduction of American and Soviet satellite surveillance in the 1960s" (Herman, 1998: 3). As it also happened, "the Cold War also made diplomacy less valuable in antagonists' monitoring of each other" (Herman, 1998: 3). In effect, American and Western European embassies based in Russia were virtually inactive, existing "in a kind of quarantine," with "reciprocal restrictions imposed on Soviet Bloc diplomats in the West" (Herman, 1998: 3). As a result of these, the diplomatic tradition of entitlement to "freedom of movement and travel" was put under abeyance by "limitations in the interests of the receiving states' 'national security'" (Herman, 1998: 3). As a result, states began to emphasise their expenditure on intelligence gathering and less on diplomatic outlets. This proved transformative for diplomacy, which had, at least since the Renaissance and the Treaty of Westphalia, been defined by information gathering and the conduct of foreign policy:

> "The overall effect is that diplomacy's traditional task of knowing foreign countries is now shared by intelligence as a complementary and potentially rival institution, of comparable weight to diplomacy in western Europe, and greater weight in America. As Sir Reginald Hibbert, a retired British diplomat, described the result: 'secret intelligence, from being a somewhat bohemian servant or associate of the great departments of state, gradually acquired a sort of parity with them'" (Herman, 1998: 4).

This has also added to the balkanisation of policymaking procedures as "apart from its small and specialized component of covert action, [intelligence's] essence is providing information and forecasts for others to act on. Unlike diplomacy, it is not a decision-taking and executive institution" (Herman, 1998: 6). Globally, international conventions also caught up with the practices. In the preceding two or so centuries, the differentiation between acceptable and unacceptable ways of acquiring information has been attempted. The illegal acquisition of information, however, has not been halted by the Vienna Convention's (1961) rather broad and ambiguous definition of the purpose of diplomacy as including "ascertaining conditions in the host country by all lawful means" which has allowed diplomats to interpret this concept as widely as possible while at the same time steering clear of explicitly breaking the laws of the host country (Herman, 1998: 7). At the same time, intelligence communities are freer and have access to methods and means not accessible to diplomats (Herman, 1998: 8). This does not give automated advantage for intelligence, however.

> "It is very rare for it to contradict what has already been deduced from non-secret information. Its great virtue is often that it gives immediacy, practicality and focus to general conclusions which have already been reached. Secret and top secret intelligence mostly has value only for very short periods. It tells you what is intended tomorrow or next week, not in the longer term. It gives you the negotiating ploy at the next meeting or the initiative which

is to be launched next month. Its value is usually tactical: strategy depends more on the picture put together from the broader, non-secret, general intelligence material" (Hibbert, 1990: 113).

This highlights that both communities need each other to successfully lend themselves to their countries' raison d'être. Furthermore, intelligence also lends itself to perception management and projection by countries. Perhaps most significant is the importance of national reputation for managing intelligence. The US is a legitimate hegemon (at least among its allies) not only for its unparalleled economic might and military budget but also for unrivalled intelligence gathering (Herman, 1998: 11). It is indeed notable that it gained its hegemonic status after WWII, after which the country emerged as one of two military superpowers but also in whose immediate aftermath it established the Central Intelligence Agency (CIA) in 1947. Before the war, America's intelligence-gathering community (under the Office of Strategic Services) had been a loose, directionless network of government departments and their informers; by 1953 it was capable of single-handedly engineering a coup in Iran. On the other hand, a national reputation of being poor at intelligence management tends to be treated as a negative indicator. For example, when West Germany was breached by East Germany at the height of the Cold War, this led to skepticism over admitting the country to the core areas of North Atlantic Treaty Organisation (NATO). One of the most active and long-lasting multi-member intelligence sharing platforms is the Five Eyes (FVEY).

The FVEY is an intelligence alliance of anglophone countries including Australia, Canada, New Zealand, the United Kingdom and the United States. These states are all parties to the 1946 UK, US and Australia (UKUSA) Agreement, establishing means for joint cooperation in signals intelligence (Hanna, 2017). Following WWII, these countries decided to maintain their successful intelligence sharing operations developed during the war more formally. The aim of the agreement is to simplify intelligence-gathering and sharing procedures among any two member states in order to more effectively avert threats stemming from rivals; in the 20th century this was the Soviet Union and in the present this increasingly appears to be Russia and China (Pfluke, 2019: 302). Recently, in 2019, technology has been at the centre of a dilemma in the alliance. At its root, the US was convinced that all alliance members should refrain from utilising devices made by Chinese tech giant (and a company with links to the Chinese government) Huawei as they could lead to sensitive information making its way to the Chinese government, a perceived adversary for the US but a country in a state of ambiguity partnership for the rest of the FVEY members (Corera, 2019).

In turn, American politicians from both the Democratic and Republican party are increasingly pondering the question of whether to allow US companies to enter the Chinese market "given the potential [unwanted] technology transfer involved" (Smith and Browne, 2019: 254). Such is the increasingly fractured state of global cooperation, in the midst of which the need for platforms for global multilateral cooperation on technology-rooted issues are increasing in scope. This is turned to in the following section.

## 8.4  Technology as a Transnational Issue

The Treaty of Pelindaba, formally termed the "African Nuclear-Weapons-Free Zone Treaty" (which was opened for signature on 11 April 1996, and entered into force in 2009), has been signed by 52 of the continent's 53 states (with 2011-established South Sudan being the only non-party to the treaty); it prohibits signatories from: "conducting research on, developing, manufacturing, stockpiling, acquiring, possessing, or having control over any nuclear explosive device by any means anywhere." The treaty was an achievement obtained through the work of the Organisation of African Unity (OAU), which had held the ideal of a nuclear-free continent since its formation in the early 1960s. Success has been more elusive on the denuclearisation of the Korean peninsula.

> "There is no alternative now to a negotiated settlement, and despite past failures, there are reasons for optimism. North Korea's leader, Chairman Kim Jong Un has declared that his strategic ambitions have been realised and that it is now time to reap the rewards. Sanctions failed to thwart the North's nuclear program but combined with misdirection of resources and poor management have crippled the North Korean economy" (Tilemann, 2018: 1).

All recognise that there will be a need to overcome ingrained trust deficits and that this will be impossible if there are no verification arrangements on an unprecedented scale. As New Threat Initiative (NTI) director John Tilemann observed: "the security dimension will need to be accompanied by economic reforms and cooperation allowing the DPRK to move from the Juche doctrine of self-sufficient isolationism, to one of engagement with its prospering neighbours" (2018: 1).

At the same time, concerns over energy and climate change have been growing. The annually released UN report *The Global E-waste Monitor* provides the most comprehensive overview of global e-waste statistics following the guidelines that were developed by the Partnership on Measuring ICT for Development. In 2017 it stated that:

> "All the countries in the world combined generated a staggering 44.7 million metric tonnes (Mt), or an equivalent of 6.1 kilogram per inhabitant (kg/inhabitant), of e-waste annually in 2016, compared to the 5.8 kg/inhabitant generated in 2014. This is close to 4,500 Eiffel Towers each year. The amount of e-waste is expected to increase to 52.2 million metric tonnes, or 6.8 kg/inh, by 2021" (Baldé, Forti, Gray, Kuehr, and Stegmann, 2017: 4).

Of those 44.7 Mt, some 1.7 Mt are thrown into the residual waste in higher-income countries and are likely to be incinerated or land-filled. Worldwide only about 8.9 Mt (or just about 20%) of e-waste are set aside to be collected and recycled. Table 8.1 provides a snapshot of the total contributions of various continents to global e-waste.

However, per inhabitant, Asia generates less e-waste per inhabitant (about 4.2 kg/inhabitant) whereas Africa generates even less (at about 1.9 kg/inhabitant) and there is scant information on collection rates for the latter (Baldé *et al.*, 2017: 6). There are a number of reasons to the growth of e-waste, but chief among these is the increase in ICT use the world over, along with shorter replacement cycles. The report observes that "the global information society" is advancing at a fast pace, defined by "an increasing number of users and rapid technological advances that are driving innovation, efficiency, and social and economic development" — but this is

Table 8.1.   Summary of total e-waste per region.

| Continent | Total e-waste in 2016 |
| --- | --- |
| Asia | 18.2 Mt |
| Europe | 12.3 Mt |
| the Americas | 11.3 Mt |
| Africa | 2.2 Mt |
| Oceania | 0.7 Mt |

*Source*: Information obtained from *The Global E-waste Monitor* 2017.

concomitant with pollution, which is set to grow with the rapid growth of the globe towards the 4IR (Baldé *et al.*, 2017: 4). By 2017, close to half the world's population used the Internet, and the majority of the people in the world have access to mobile networks and services. Indeed, many people across the world have ownership of more than one ICT device. This is because of growths in disposable incomes in the developing world, resulting in a growing global middle-class that is able to purchase more electronic products leading to heightened waste (Baldé *et al.*, 2017: 4):

> "Increasing levels of electronic waste, and its improper and unsafe treatment and disposal through open burning or in dumpsites, pose significant risks to the environment and human health. They also present several challenges to sustainable development, and to the achievement of the Sustainable Development Goals" (Baldé *et al.*, 2017: 3).

The problem of e-waste is one that will require participation by both state and non-governmental actors as these increasingly "engage as relative equals with states" (Bousfield, 2017: 1047). In the realm of diplomacy, this has garnered the label of cyber-diplomacy, "which would supplant international theoretical framings of geopolitics (realist, liberal, Marxist, etc.) with media theory and the social power of ICTs" (Deibert, 2002: 38). In early conceptions, cyber-diplomacy was primarily framed as "how diplomacy is adapting to the new global information order," retaining a state centric framing as "technologically oriented diplomacy" (Potter, 2002: 7). This has led to the establishment, for example, of the office of the first Tech Ambassador in Denmark in 2017, whose office is to be "responsible for connecting the Danish government to tech companies around the world" (Smith and Browne, 2019: 109). Though the first such office, it was on the example of the British government's own decision in 2014 to designate a "special envoy to US technology companies" occupied by Sir Nigel Sheinwald, a former UK ambassador to the US (Smith and Browne, 2019: 109).

In many ways, this was in recognition of the pre-existing record of non-state actors participating and indeed leading in transnational issues. A variety of international non-governmental organizations (INGOs) have been influential, most recently in the International Campaign to Ban Landmines 1990s, which was started by six international non-governmental organizations in 1992 and came to involve about 1,000 others, active in 60 countries. The group "successfully reframed landmines into a humanitarian and moral issue, rather than a purely military matter" and upon gaining support from the Canadian government moved up its campaign to an *ad hoc* forum that in 1997 adopted a landmine ban treaty (Smith and Browne, 2019: 127). This has all the markings of a post-Westphalian order, indicating power residing in a multiplicity of multilateral actors including sub-national actors such as cities and provinces, companies, INGOs, and even individuals. In this post-Westphalian world, in particular, "the pervasive nature of information and communications technology increasingly thrusts the tech sector into the center of foreign policy issues" (Smith and Browne, 2019: 110).

Michael Scott Moore argues against international treaties that are modeled on examples such as chemical-weapons agreements which would ostensibly aim to establish "cyberpeace" only between and among nations as this process would be dominated by the interests and sensitivities of big, powerful states. Moreover, it may become effectively biased against non-state actors and render citizens vulnerable to being spied on by their own governments, while such treaties would remain ineffective against hackers with superior capabilities (Moore, 2017). As seen in preceding chapters, national interests — or regional interests in the case of the EU — stand poised to shape emerging technologies.

In 2020, with the COVID-19 pandemic having ground international travel to a halt, the nearly 75-year old tradition of world leaders assembling in New York City in September was temporarily paused. Instead, world leaders participated, for the first time ever, through virtual platforms. Soon the Presidency of the Russian Federation decided that it would host the eight member Shanghai Cooperation Organisation (SCO) of primarily Asian states as well as the BRICS summit online. Similarly Saudi Arabia, in its capacity as the president of G-20 decided to host the summit in similar fashion after making intense efforts to host it in physical format (Chaudhury, 2020). Is this the likely future of the United Nations and other platforms of international summitry? Might we also see war reparations being paid through blockchain in the form of cryptocurrencies, or donations to poor countries through 3D printing? Experts are of the view that physical summits are indispensable and will remain so: "the summits held physically have huge significance as meetings on sidelines help leaders build chemistry and give direction to policies" report the *Economic Times of India* after speaking to officials in the Presidency of India following the decision to participate in the virtual platform (Chaudhury, 2020). They would have preferred to have the physical meetings with the leaders of the two countries meeting with one another, especially in light of recent tensions over their border. While this is not likely to be a permanent state of affairs, we do anticipate a scaling down of delegations and in-person meetings by populous working groups while delegations may become smaller as hybrid diplomatic engagements become the norm. Embassies and foreign affairs departments the world over have embarked on technological readiness precisely with this in mind. This may especially be the case as countries embark on cost-cutting measures in pursuit of post-COVID recovery. Moreover, the advancements in AI present ample opportunities for new standards of objectivity to be utilised by the United Nations. In addition to a World Health Organisation (WHO) task team on finding ways to globalise the uses of AI in healthcare decision making, the International Atomic Energy Agency (IAEA) could find ways to infuse AI into its nuclear verification procedures and the International Court of Justice (ICJ) could benefit from the use of such programmes in arbitrating disputes before it. Nevertheless, this would still require human decision making and would only attain legitimacy after reaching a certain threshold. Moreover, it would require near-universal endorsement, itself a very political process given the likely differences in axioms and starting points for such programmes. Questions may also arise as to the origins and production of such algorithms in addition to skepticism over security.

As a result of this, it would appear that the advances being made in AI and other emerging technologies are likely to only expand the diplomatic lexicon and work alongside members of the diplomatic corps rather than supplant the diplomatic process with AI specialists and other technocrats. This has been seen, for example, in so-called areas of track II diplomacy including transport diplomacy (observed by South Africa's use of railroads and access to its harbours to gain the cooperation of countries of other landlocked African states), sports diplomacy (seen in the tendency of countries playing host to FIFA and the Olympics to use such status to broaden their image), panda diplomacy (seen in China's renting out of its indigenous panda species to countries it seeks deeper cooperation), and gastro diplomacy (seen in countries' use of food and culture as levers of soft power). Nevertheless, these are prognostications based on contemporary evidence at the early phase of the 4IR. The history of technology informs us, however, that the relationship between the international diplomatic forums and emerging technologies is bound to ratchet further — they are inventions in search of applications. The relationship is also bidirectional and can, at the very least, lead to findings on aspects of the diplomatic process and the forums which ensconce it. Already, it has been noted how Google Translate, having been initially based on a corpus of United Nations and European parliament documentation, has led to an English-leaning bias (Tanner, 2007). This is to the detriment of thousands of other languages, many of which are not yet incorporated into the platform (Marwala, 2020: 164). Given grievances over the need to reform the United Nations, these emerging technologies can reveal nuances of the UN's inherent biases and, in the process, perhaps also shed light on new ways out. This is a phenomenon termed the double hermeneutic in the social sciences. Quite simply, this refers to the process by which our introduction of new systems has the potential to reveal new information about our world which can allow us to remake it favourably; to be more inclusive and more efficient. This is but one promise of the 4IR that will nonetheless be realised through concerted and collective action by the international community.

# References

Adesina, Olubukola S. 2017. "Foreign policy in an era of digital diplomacy," *Cogent Social Sciences*, 3(1), 1–13. DOI: http://dx.doi.org/10.1080/23311886.2017.1297175.

Balde, Cornelis P., Forti, Vanessa, Gray, Vanessa, Kuehr, Ruediger, and Stegmann. Paul. 2017. *The Global E-waste Monitor 2017*. Bonn, Geneva and Vienna: United Nations University, International Telecommunication Union and the International Solid Waste Association.

Bousfield, Dan. 2017. "Revisiting Cyber-Diplomacy: Canada–China Relations Online," *Globalizations*, 14(6), 1045–1059.

Chaudhury, Dipanjan Roy. 2020. "2020: The year of virtual summits amid global pandemic," *Economic Times of India*. URL: https://economictimes.india times.com/news/politics-and-nation/2020-the-year-of-virtual-summits-amid- global-pandemic/articleshow/78368767.cms?utm_source= contentofinterest &utm_medium=text&utm_campaign=cppst (Accessed: 14 November 2020).

Corera, Gordon. 2019 (February 20). "Could Huawei threaten the Five Eyes alliance?," *BBC*. URL: https://www.bbc.com/news/technology-47305420 (Accessed: 3 January 2020).

Deibert, R. 2002. "Hyper-Realities of world politics: Theorizing the communications revolution," in E. Potter (Ed.), *Cyber-Diplomacy: Managing Foreign Policy in the Twenty-First Century* (pp. 27–47), Montreal: McGill-Queen's Press.

Department of International Relations and Cooperation (South Africa). 2019. *Foreign Policy Review: Strategic Reflection and Critical Appraisal of the Orientation and Implementation of South Africa's Foreign Policy*. Pretoria: Government Gazette.

Hanna, Jason. 2017. "What is the Five Eyes intelligence pact?," *BBC*. URL: https://edition.cnn.com/2017/05/25/world/uk-us-five-eyes-intelligence-explai ner/index.html (Accessed: 3 January 2020).

Herman, Michael. 1998. "Diplomacy and intelligence," *Diplomacy and Statecraft*, 9(2), 1–22.

Hibbert, Reginald. 1990. "Intelligence and Policy," *Intelligence and National Security*, 5(1), 110–128.

Krasnyak, Olga. 2018 (December 13). "National Styles in Science Diplomacy: China," USC Center on Public Diplomacy. URL: https://www.uscpublic diplomacy.org/blog/national-styles-science-diplomacy-china (Last accessed: 3 January 2020).

Marwala, Tshilidzi. 2020. "Chapter 19: Languages," in *Closing the Gap*. Johannesburg: Macmillan.

Moore, Michael Scott. 2017 (May 3). "International Treaties and the Internet," *Pacific Standard*. URL: https://psmag.com/news/international-treaties-and-the-internet-22622 (Accessed: 14 November 2020).

Pandor, Naledi. 2012 (March 9). "South African Science Diplomacy: Fostering Global Partnerships and Advancing the African Agenda," *Science and Diplomacy*. URL: http://www.sciencediplomacy.org/perspective/2012/south-african-science-diplomacy (Accessed: 3 January 2020).

Pfluke, Corey. 2019. "A history of the Five Eyes Alliance: Possibility for reform and additions," *Comparative Strategy*, 38(4), 302–315.

Potter, E. 2002. *Cyber-Diplomacy: Managing Foreign Policy in the Twenty-First Century*. Montreal: McGill-Queen's University Press.

Rashica, Viona. 2018. "The Benefits and Risks of Digital Diplomacy," *SEEU Review*, 13(1): 75–89.

Roig, Alexis (2018). Towards a city-led Science Diplomacy: The rise of cities in a multilateral world and their role in a science-driven global governance. UNITAR. URL: http://www.scitechdiplohub.org/what-is-science-diplomacy/ (Accessed: 3 January 2020).

Schjolberg, Stein. 2010. "A Cyberspace Treaty – A United Nations Convention or Protocol on Cybersecurity and Cybercrime," Twelfth United Nations Congress on Crime Prevention and Criminal Justice (Salvador, Brazil, 12–19 April).

Serrano, Antonio Segura. 2019. "International Regulation of the Internet," *Oxford Bibliographies*. URL: https://www.oxfordbibliographies.com/view/document/obo-9780199796953/obo-9780199796953-0194.xml (Accessed: 3 January 2020).

Smith, Brad and Browne, Carol Ann. 2019. *Tools and Weapons: The Promise and the Peril of the Digital Age*. London: Hodder and Stoughton.

Tanner, Adam. 2007 (March 28). "Google seeks world of instant translations," *Reuters*. URL: https://www.reuters.com/article/us-google-translate-idUSN1921881520070328 (Accessed: 14 November 2020).

The Royal Society. 2010 (January). "New frontiers in science diplomacy," The Royal Society. URL: https://royalsociety.org/~/media/Royal_Society_Content/policy/publications/2010/4294969468.pdf (Accessed: 3 January 2020).

Tilemann, John. 2018 (June 7). "Policy Brief No 64 — Korean Peninsula Nuclear Summitry: The Time is Right," Asia-Pacific Leadership Network for Nuclear

Non-Proliferation and Disarmament. URL: http://www.apln.network/briefings/ briefings_view/Policy_Brief_No_64_-_Korean_Peninsula_Nuclear_Summitry: _The_Time_is_Right (Accessed: 3 January 2020).

United Nations Conference on Trade and Development. 2003 (January 31). "Science and Technology Diplomacy: Concepts and Elements of a Work Programme," United Nations. URL: https://unctad.org/en/docs/itetebmisc5_en. pdf (Accessed: 3 January 2020).

Yakushiji, Taizo. 2009. "The Potential of Science and Technology Diplomacy," *Asia-Pacific Review*, 16(1), 1–7.

# Conclusion: Towards an International Relations Technology Research Agenda

# 9

**Abstract**

This chapter concludes the book by synthesising its key findings. Moreover, we point out areas for further research around the future of globalisation, development, intellectual property, war. democracy, the nature of techno-logical asymmetries and their implications and policy imperatives, oppor-tunities for theoretical updating, and the relative merits of quantitative and qualitative analysis.

**Keywords**: Artificial intelligence; fourth industrial revolution; machine learning

## 9.1  Introduction

This book set out to reflect a survey of the literature on technology dynamics in international politics and international political economy and note some emerging themes on the role of technology in the areas of public policy as it relates to foreign direct investment flows, the relationships between infrastructure, industrialisation and development, as well as in war, regional integration and the international diplomatic arena. Considering the currents found in the literature, this Conclusion briefly considers the implications of machine learning, the major difference maker of today's AI landscape compared to previous epochs, and subsequently notes some areas for further research to consolidate and further deepen the field of IR as it relates to and takes cognisance of technology dynamics.

In an estimate by PriceWaterhouseCoopers (2019), AI contributes about US$2 trillion to today's global economy and is predicted to reach some US$16 trillion by 2030 (roughly 10% of world current GDP) given growth in patent applications — being the third fastest-growing category of all patents granted and representing nearly 60% of all new investment in AI. In light of the very welcome growth in analyses of ongoing technological changes and what they mean for IR, it is worth unpacking the ongoing and future implications of this particular technology on its own and apart from other technologies, including other facets of modern AI.

Machine learning looks set to change the nature of globalisation. One of the features of globalisation has been the constant importation of, usually, Western-developed technologies which are subsequently retrospectively fitted into the local contexts of various non-Western societies. ML stands to possibly fix this through correcting the generally ahistorical nature of new technologies. In other words, technologies and other data-based products (and even services) can be pre-modulated to local contexts. This can curtail costs for businesses in the long-term and presents opportunities for true "glocalization" for companies that can develop or adopt ML. Being autonomous but operating within a centralised network (Big Data) with real-time learning, ML could lead to a new face of globalisation; with multinational corporations (MNCs), embassies, international non-governmental organisations (NGOs), transnational advocacy networks (TANs) and other international state- and non-state actors acting on the basis of fresh, relevant and objectively obtained data. In the short to medium-term, depending on the pace of development of fully-fledged unsupervised machine learning, ML will be a job creator for the literate and semi-skilled. For any ML to be able to operate in a relevant manner, it needs to interface digitally with the physical world, and for that they need annotation. Essentially referring to the process of making programs recognise the physical environment, annotation requires painstaking labelling of the physical world. This makes it a job creator as this is a process which cannot be done from afar and needs local participation. Amazon's Mechanical Turk (MTurk) for example is based on reaching out to globally distributed workers who perform labelling for supervised machine learning. Moreover, it necessarily cannot be automated in the early stages. Many enthusiasts and Internet sleuths have generated compilations of programmes mislabeling muffins as dogs. This is serious stuff, however. Recent emphases on diversity are driven by the need for unbiased algorithms. Recent embarrassments — such as Google's Data Cloud labelling of the same object differently held by an Asian and African American as a calculator and as a gun respectively — demonstrate that calls for diversity are not just matters of symbolism but can be fatal incidents and thus lend credence to the importance of geographically diverse inputs. Mishandled, algorithms could lead to fatal interactions between law enforcement and members of the community. Employment creation is an inescapable by-product of this, as inputs about local surroundings cannot be substituted or outsourced.

One recent AI initiative to stem from South Africa has been Enlabeler, which was initiated by Cape Town-based developer Pieter Boon. Enlabeler is a data labelling platform "powered" (in its own terminology) by people living in the township of Khayelitsha who form part of its team and conduct its data annotation, data structuring and data labelling to a global clientele. This should incentivise investment in literacy in order to attract companies in need of annotators. In this way the global becomes the local. Annotating, however, is not a long-term strategy as it could be potentially time-bound as the bulk of the labelling may be done on a once-off basis. A 2019 Carnegie report, for example, observes that despite a nominally low barrier to entry, demand is likely to increase mainly in those countries that have a high rate of English speakers. Moreover, local start-ups may be bought up by larger firms eager to consolidate their positions in the field. Such was the case with DeepMind, founded in the UK in 2010 and subsequently bought out by Google in 2014 for a reported US$500 million.

ML can also transform the global economy through impacting how we conceive of the process of technology transfers. Quite possibly, it can catalyse and facilitate the process and can make it more meaningful. Domestic absorptive capacity, however, remains key. This highlights the question of incentives; for the governments to create such conducive ecosystems, and for the foreign tech companies to want to participate in the tech transfer when they could be better positioned to understand the local conditions and thus require little to no partnership with local companies. The latter being one of the key predictors of engagement in tech transfer, it necessitates protection mechanisms as foreign MNCs may end up knowing more than local governments and communities about their own populations' behavioural patterns.

## 9.2 Themes for Future Research

### 9.2.1 *Long Peace, Technology and the Future of War*

Firstly, if war is politics by other means, and indeed remains impervious to (and indeed co-opts) transformations in technology as argued by Carl von Clausewitz and his followers, future research could more directly draw points of similarity between wars from across eras while also tracing and isolating for the character and effect of new technologies in those conflicts. Secondly, noting what some scholars (e.g., Goldstein [2012] and Pinker [2011]) have termed a long peace in terms of inter-state conflict in the post-Cold War era, scholars could distil what role technology has played in limiting the number and magnitude of inter-state conflicts in the present era and determine the precise role of AI in the future of war. Future research could also more critically engage the relevance of deterrence in the contemporary international context. Third, there is benefit to be gained from conducting a survey of the next global conflict, which could take into account for the role of technology in such a confrontation (or sets of confrontations) on a global scale in terms of the likely actors, casualties and winners or losers. Alternatively, is technology likely to make such an outbreak less possible?

### 9.2.2  *Democracy*

Given the recent trends in technologies interfacing with voting and campaigns, investigators can determine whether, and by how much, the emerging technologies such as Big Data, AI, and blockchain technology, promote or undermine democracy through succinct and objective metrics as well as methods for determining causation and attribution of responsibility.

### 9.2.3  *Assymetries and Their Implications*

Future research should determine what consequences are being seen or are likely to be seen as a result of the global inequality in technological asymmetries. Are we set to see more populism or can policies be put into place to expedite new forms of economic participation? Furthermore, in light of the emerging and potential-laden field of new materials (as well as the distant but advancing area of asteroid mining), economic modelling can be used to demonstrate and predict what the likely effects of revolutions in mineral extraction on resource-dependent economies are, and how they can be responded to.

### 9.2.4  *Theoretical Updating*

Given the nature of the advances being made in AI and its manifestation in areas relevant to IR, and the impact these are having on a number of its underlining assumptions, its theoretical paradigms may be in need of updating. To these ends, this future research should investigate the implications of the increasing interface between AI and various aspects of IR. We should examine and where appropriate update liberalism, realism, hegemonic stability theory, world systems theory and the English School of International Relations (with its focus on the notion of the global landscape as being composed of "a society of states").

### 9.2.5  *Quantitative and Qualitative Analysis*

Fifth, scholars could weigh up the comparative merits and demerits of quantitative and qualitative methodologies in researching the human–technology nexus in the field. Which methodology is best for which specific research agenda and, where relevant and deemed appropriate, how can they be integrated?

### 9.2.6  *Intellectual Property Ownership*

Finally, future research can survey the technological landscape in terms of the key multinational corporations, noting the nature of technological ownership in the 21st century in terms of these actors, with reference to continuities and changes in the custodianship and stewardship of technology as well as the public-private dimension. What legal measures and mechanisms exist to both enable and restrain MNCs in the technological sector?

While no single work in these and many other emerging areas will be definitive, each in relation and in response to the other will make a contribution to the related fields and in the process further entrench the growing and highly needed inter-disciplinary work. This is especially necessitated by the disciplinary overlaps and crossovers in our early context which are set, all other things being equal, to only continue to grow.

### References

Goldstein, Joshua S. 2012. *Winning the War on War: The Decline of Armed Conflict Worldwide*. New York: Plume.

Pinker, Steven. 2011. *The Better Angels of Our Nature: Why Violence Has Declined*. New York: Viking Books.

PriceWaterhouseCoopers. 2019. "PwC's Global Artificial Intelligence Study: Exploiting the AI Revolution," PriceWaterhouseCoopers. URL: https://www.pwc.com/gx/en/issues/data-and-analytics/publications/artificial-intelligence-study.html (Accessed: 1 November 2020).

# Index

Printed in the United States
by Baker & Taylor Publisher Services